SEXUAL HARASSMENT
HIGH SCHOOL GIRLS SPEAK OUT

SEXUAL HARASSMENT

HIGH SCHOOL
GIRLS
SPEAK OUT

JUNE LARKIN

SECOND STORY Press

CANADIAN CATALOGUING IN PUBLICATION DATA

Larkin, June, 1952-
Sexual harassment : high school girls speak out

ISBN 0-929005-65-1

1. Sexual harassment in education. I. Title.

LC212.8.L37 1994   370.19'345   C94-932385-3

Second printing 1997

Edited by Sarah Silberstein Swartz

Printed and bound in Canada

Second Story Press gratefully acknowledges the assistance
of the *Ontario Arts Council* and *The Canada Council*

Published by
SECOND STORY PRESS
720 Bathurst Street Suite 301
Toronto, Ontario
M5S 2R4

For my mother,
Evelyn Tremblay Larkin

"The wind beneath my wings."

CONTENTS

ACKNOWLEDGMENTS

THE COMPLETION OF THIS WORK has been a collaborative effort. Throughout this project I have had around me a supportive group of friends, colleagues, and family members who have been generous with their time, encouragement and understanding. I am truly indebted to them.

Above all, I wish to express my gratitude to Paula Caplan. She is truly an inspiration. Her careful guidance and tireless mentoring have made the completion of this work an empowering experience. Words cannot express my appreciation for all she has taught me. As this project comes to a close, I am honoured to know her not only as teacher but, more importantly, as friend.

I am grateful to Cara Bennison, Eimear O'Neill and Evelyn Tremblay Larkin for the thoughtful and, often, immediate feedback they provided as I progressed in this work. I would also like to thank the following people who provided valuable comments on earlier versions of this manuscript: Kay Armatage, Lisa Gotell, Toni Laidlaw, Marion Lynn, Angela Miles, Milana Todoroff and Jeri Wine.

Working with Second Story Press has been a wonderful experience. Margie Wolfe and Sarah Swartz, in particular, have assisted me in so many ways. Their support has helped to make the writing of this book an enjoyable task.

I am also grateful to the London and Middlesex Roman Catholic School Board for granting me the time I needed to complete this project. I can only hope that our students and educators will benefit from the work I have done.

I would also like to acknowledge the Social Science and Humanities Research Council of Canada who provided the funding that allowed me to get this project off the ground. Their financial endorsement was, I believe, a statement of their belief in the value of this work.

And, of course, I am indebted to the teachers and students who participated in this project but whose names cannot be listed here, in order to protect their privacy. I admire their courage. I can only hope that they will reap the benefits of having been pioneers in the process of making schools better places for young women.

To my family, Mom, Kathy, Nancy, Trevor, Julie, Sara, and Garrett and my friends, Alison, Bev, Bette, Carole Ann, Christabelle, Clara, Corrie, Debbie, Diane, Fatima, Gay, Helen, Hilary, Joy, Kathryn, Linda, Marina, Moira, Pat, Patience, John, Judy, Moji, Rosie, Sharon, Teresa, Tony, Val and Vlasta who have provided unfailing moral support over the past few months. Thank you. You have carried me through the rough but exhilarating final steps of a life-long goal.

—J. L.

PREFACE

SINCE THE PUBLICATION of *Sexual Harassment: High School Girls Speak Out* in 1994, I have worked with educators, students and parents across Canada on the problem of school-based sexual harassment. The response has been encouraging. No doubt, there is some degree of polite attention and reluctant tolerance by those who are not convinced of the severity of the problem. But the wrenching stories of young women worn down by persistent and pervasive sexual and gender hassling have a familiar ring for most students and adults. Many have added their personal accounts to the litany of harassing acts I have documented in my own research.

A disturbing trend is the increasing stories of vicious verbal assaults by female students who are using harassment to move up the domination hierarchy. Small wonder. Girls who have experienced the sting of gendered insults firsthand have a visceral understanding of the strength and potency of language. Engaging in verbal warfare and other abusive practices may seem like the natural route to equality for those who have felt the bitter connection between violence and power. Unless we stop thinking about power in terms of winners and losers, more and more girls will try to bully their way to equity by adopting the demeaning behaviour that has worked so well against them. As one young woman put it, "If girls can't get equal, they'll try to get even."

When I do sexual harassment talks and workshops with educators, I am typically asked to provide a list of strategies for dealing with harassing incidents. This is a reasonable request. We need ways to handle the routine and extreme forms of harassment that occur in schools. But focusing on isolated incidents of sexual harassment is a simplistic Band-Aid solution to a serious and complex problem.

To deal effectively with sexual harassment, we need to move beyond a "quick-fix" or "bag of tricks" approach and consider, instead, the systemic nature of the problem: the ways the very structure of our educational system create a climate that fosters harassment and other forms of abuse against females and other marginalized groups. This means exposing and confronting the subtle, and not so subtle, ways that sexism, racism, classism, homophobia and other discriminatory practices shape the school curriculum and our interactions with students. Taking this integrated and multi-faceted approach is important. The experience of sexual harassment can be deeply wounding for any young woman, but the impact is compounded for students who do not have the buffer of race and class privilege.

Going beyond the "quick-fix" approach to dealing with sexual harassment means providing systemic responses to the problem. Educators can begin by examining their curriculum content and classroom practices for gender bias. Who takes up most verbal space in the classroom? What groups of people are highlighted in the curriculum? Do males and females have equal access to computers and other resources?

The humiliation of sexual harassment starts early. Over the past couple of years, I have become convinced that sexual harassment must be checked in elementary schools if we are ever going to make headway in eliminating the problem. Complaints about primary girls being called "sluts" and "bitches" by their male classmates are pretty standard. Often, the abuse escalates. One grade 7 girl attempted suicide in a desperate attempt to avoid facing her male classmates and their relentless harassment which, over the school year, had been stepped up from ordinary gendered put-downs to threats of sexual assault. When the principal investigated, he learned that the same boys had terrorized other female students who had determined that silence was their best bet for escaping serious harm.

Hats off to the hundreds of educators who are providing students with alternatives to the "grin and bear it" strategy for dealing with sexually harassing behaviour. By confronting the problem of sexual harassment in schools, we are beginning to chip away at a major barrier to girls' education. In the process, we are meeting the equity challenge by creating schools that are positive and supportive places for *all* students.

June Larkin August 1997

INTRODUCTION

I really hate going to this class because where I sit I'm surrounded by guys and they keep talking about hookers, strip bars, women's body parts, "making it" with girls, and so on. It really makes me angry. It makes me sick to my stomach.

A lot of girls won't walk down school hallways 'cause they know guys will be there grabbing their arms or saying, "Oh, come here baby." Most girls won't walk through a particular hallway because of the gestures.

A guy held a girl up to her locker and made her stay there while he kicked her.

In some of my classes the guys embarrass you and mostly in front of everybody. So in class the first month or so, I'd be quiet really quiet. If they're quiet and they don't do anything, then later I can talk.

I was sitting in class and the guys behind me kept flipping my skirt. When I turned around to tell them to stop the teacher yelled at me. I tried to tell her what they were doing but she told me to be quiet and stop interrupting the class.

This one teacher always says horrible things about women. He doesn't think a woman can do anything.

For many female students, stories like these are depressingly routine. The consequences can be devastating, as young women struggle to survive in a learning environment they often experience as toxic. When so much of a female student's day is spent fending off diminishing comments, sexual innuendos, and physical pestering, how can she be expected to thrive at school?

In writing this book, I want to make visible the unexpressed suffering of so many female students and provide resources and strategies for educators who want to deal with it. Tackling the problem of sexual harassment in schools may be the key to providing equal education for girls, because it is one of the most powerful forces working against female students. In this book, young women speak out about the sexual harassment that is part of the fabric of their school life and they describe how this behaviour affects their education.

In May 1994, Marion Boyd, Ontario Women's Issues Minister, raised public awareness about the problem of sexual harassment in schools, when she held a news conference to launch a $415,000 sexual assault awareness program. Her comments highlighted the inextricable link between sexual harassment and other forms of sexual violence against women. According to Boyd, sexual assault is learned at a young age and begins when school-age boys start calling girls cows, pigs, sluts and other derogatory names. Such verbal abuse, when unchecked, can lead to degrading acts such as boys lifting up girls' skirts, thrusting their hands between girls' legs or holding them down in mock intercourse.[1] The tendency in the past has been to dismiss much of this demeaning behaviour as nothing more than "boys will be boys" kind of antics. But it's only a small step from mock intercourse to actual rape and we all make way for this progression when we tolerate the many ways males diminish females.

If we consider all the attention given to equal opportunity in education, it is curious that so little attention has been given to the sexual harassment girls experience in school and the ways this behaviour interferes with their education.

During my career as an elementary school teacher, I had always considered myself a strong proponent of equal education for girls; I talked about female scientists, told feminist fairytales, covered my walls with posters about the accomplishments of girls and women and made a conscious attempt to use inclusive language. But I hadn't even thought about sexual harassment as an issue of equal opportunity until I left teaching and became a graduate student at the Ontario Institute for Studies in Education (OISE).

There, through my work with the Women's Caucus Against Sexual Harassment, I heard never-ending accounts of the put-downs, threats and sexual overtures suffered by adult women. I learned how they had adjusted their academic and/or career plans because of this behaviour. Some women had quit jobs; others had dropped courses or changed universities. But it wasn't until my friend's daughter, a high school student, told me of her experiences — being rated on a scale of one to ten by male students, being pinched and grabbed and invited to join a group of young men in the back of a van, and sitting in a classroom where a teacher continually reminded his students that women really do belong barefoot and pregnant in the kitchen — that I began to wonder to what extent the experience of sexual harassment had altered the lives of girls and young women *before* they became adults.

My commitment to examining this problem in high schools was clinched when I received the following letter from researchers involved in a number of projects centred around child abuse policy and prevention issues. They wrote:

> As part of a funded province-wide project examining Child Abuse policy and policy implementation among boards we completed interviews and administered questionnaires to a sample of teachers: male and female. During these administrations, it was not our intent to collect data around harassment issues; however both male and female teachers, at the secondary level particularly, raised

harassment concerns — especially regarding harassment of senior female students by male teachers .... . Most teachers who mentioned it appeared distressed that this is occurring and that there appears to be no means of addressing this issue.[2]

Recognizing that teachers who are entrusted with the education of female students are the perpetrators of such abusive behaviour was, of course, disturbing. But when I thought back to my own experience, I began to recall incidents committed by school officials that I hadn't labelled as sexual harassment: a principal who referred to female students as cows and a male teacher who constantly propositioned his female students are just two examples. Being harassed at school by male students can be a distressing experience, but the impact of being put-down or propositioned by a school official is even more crushing. Sometimes the consequences are irrevocable.

We can't continue to push female students forward without acknowledging all the ways they get set back. Unless we confront the problem of sexual harassment in schools, our lofty statements about providing gender equitable education are meaningless. Harassment is a major barrier to girls' education.

But most equal opportunity initiatives don't even acknowledge that sexual harassment exists. For the most part, girls are being urged into math and science, coaxed into assertiveness training, plugged into leadership courses, and remediated for their alleged cognitive deficiencies, all in the name of equal opportunity. Meanwhile, incidents of sexual harassment persist as a way of reminding them that they are not considered equal at all. This puts female students in an ambivalent situation as they grapple with the feelings of frustration, fear, rage and humiliation that arise from the demeaning behaviour they so often experience in the setting that is being lauded as their gateway to opportunity: school. Despite all the efforts directed towards equal opportunity, we know that girls' self-esteem, confidence and career aspirations continue to decrease as they progress in their education.[3] The important question is: How is this related to the harassment they receive in school? This is what I wanted to examine by interviewing the female students themselves.

My study was conducted with young women from four high schools which were selected because the school administrators had expressed an interest in doing education on sexual harassment. Before I interviewed the students, I asked them to keep a journal of their sexual harassment incidents during the school term. I arranged monthly meetings so they could share their experiences with other young women. This was the first opportunity most students had to talk about sexual harassment and their discussions generated the questions I later asked in the interviews. I structured the study this way because I wanted to be sure the information I collected in the interviews was grounded in the students' experiences, not on my own pre-conceived notions.

The students I interviewed were from schools in urban, rural and small town settings and represented a variety of racial, cultural and economic backgrounds. Such a diverse sample was important because I wanted to understand the various ways sexual harassment gets played out in young women's lives. What is the effect of sexual harassment on young women of colour who are also dealing with the every-day racism that permeates their lives? If a young women has limited economic resources, will sexual harassment be one more factor that discourages her from pursuing a higher edu-cation? These kinds of questions are key to getting a picture of the broader context of young women's lives.

Over sixty students participated in the study in some way. Most attended the group sessions; some also kept journals and/or agreed to be interviewed. Although the students varied in age, I only interviewed those who were sixteen or older because I wanted to ensure them that the information they shared with me would be confidential. I couldn't offer this assurance to students under sixteen because I would be legally obligated to report any incident of abuse they might disclose during our interview. In total, I interviewed twenty-five students.

Most of the accounts recorded here are those of the students with whom I conducted in-depth interviews. In some places, I have also included the comments of young women I interviewed prior to and following the project.

The overall goal of this book is to help educators, parents and students understand and deal with the sexual harassment that goes on in schools. The poignant comments of these young women provide shocking evidence of the hazardous conditions in which female students are trying to get an education. This book is written as a resource for those who want to make schools healthier places for girls.

In Chapter One, I discuss the meaning of the term "sexual harassment" and examine sexual harassment at school in the larger context of a sexist society which tolerates and condones the diminishment and abuse of women. In Chapter Two, I describe sexual harassment as a form of gender bias that hasn't received much attention. This is because the focus of most equal opportunity initiatives has been geared to "fixing" female students with little consideration about the ways they are treated in schools. Chapter Three outlines the process by which young women came to recognize sexual harassment as a problem and describes how the young women's thinking about sexual harassment changed when they had the opportunity to share common experiences. In Chapter Four the young women speak out about their incidents of sexual harassment by male peers and in Chapter Five they describe how this behaviour affects their education. In the final chapter, I provide educational resources and strategies for dealing with sexual harassment in schools.

Chapter One

BARRIERS TO EQUAL EDUCATION

ALTHOUGH THE TERM "sexual harassment" has only recently been coined, sexually harassing behaviour is not a new phenomenon. As early as 1911, the National Women's Trade Union League complained about the abusive and insulting language that female workers endured from men in their jobs, but they had no label for this behaviour.[1] Over eighty years later, despite the public discussion of sexual harassment which has been fuelled by such high profile cases as the Hill-Clarence hearings, many women are still reluctant to link the term "sexual harassment" to the degrading and demeaning behaviour they so often encounter in their own lives.

In October 1991, millions of North American's watched as the US media focused on Anita Hill, an African-American law professor, who went before a panel of white male senators to make public her accusations of sexual harassment against Clarence Thomas, an African-American conservative who was George Bush's nominee for the Supreme Court. Hill was labelled conniving, vindictive and psychotic (among other things) by right-wing senators and many other North Americans. In the end, Thomas's nomination to the Supreme Court was approved.

The backlash faced by Anita Hill and so many women who have dared to speak out about sexual harassment effectively silences others who worry about the consequences of making an issue about behaviour that is so often dismissed as "a joke," "natural male bravado" or "just a bit of fun." When university professor Carol Ramazanoglu protested the demeaning comments and patronizing put-downs she got from some of the men in her department, she was labelled a crank, a freak, an unprofessional, a totalitarian fascist and was ostracized by her colleagues. The cost of her speaking out about sexual harassment was more harassment.[2] Understandably, few women are willing to pay such a price. As a result, the range of what is recognized as sexually harassing behaviour gets narrowed; those acts that aren't extreme forms of sexual abuse are too often discounted.

The students I interviewed had adopted this limited notion of sexual harassment; many said they were familiar with the term "sexual harassment" but until they participated in the study they assumed it meant rape or sexual assault. After speaking with other young women at our meetings, they changed their thinking about sexual harassment, realizing how often they were in fact sexually harassed and how their own experiences of sexual harassment were similar to those of other female students.

Sexual harassment is generally defined as unwanted and unwelcomed behaviour of a sexual nature.[3] This definition is necessarily ambiguous because of the numerous factors that need to be taken into consideration: the tone of voice, the body language, the context in which the behaviour is elicited, the impact on the recipient and the power dynamics, to name a few. I didn't give the young women I interviewed a definition of sexual harassment because I wanted them to interpret the term in relation to their own experiences. I encouraged them instead to record incidents they thought might be sexual harassment. Then they shared their comments in group meetings.

When I asked the young women to define sexual harassment after they had met in groups a few times, each student had broadened the range of what she considered to be sexually harassing behaviour. Joan synthesized the various responses in this way:

> It's more than rape; it's more than just sexual assault. Sexual harassment is something that makes you feel uncomfortable about who you are ... because of the sex you are.

This definition is stripped of the legal jargon that can be so confusing and, at the same time, it is an accurate description of what sexual harassment is: unwelcome and intrusive behaviour of a sexual nature. When I work with students, teachers and educators on the problem of sexual harassment in schools, I often begin with Joan's definition.

SEXUAL HARASSMENT IN A PATRIARCHAL SOCIETY

Sexual harassment is an expression of sexism which reflects and reinforces the unequal power that exists between men and women in our patriarchal society. It's part of a pattern of male-female interaction in which men routinely express their dominance over women.

The concept of sexual harassment as an instrument of male power is in sharp contrast to the popular interpretation of males' harassing behaviour as being nothing more than a natural expression of masculinity. After speaking to educators on the topic of sexual harassment, I was approached by a superintendent of one School Board who claimed he was horrified to hear about the ways girls were being treated in schools. "But," he lamented, "there's not much you can do with boys when those male hormones start kicking in." No wonder concerned educators in this school district were having such a hard time getting administrative support for the development of a sexual harassment policy that covered students.

Historically, men's control over women was assured because women were confined to the home sphere as wives and mothers whose primary purpose was servicing the needs of men and children. When female students today are still told that women should "get back in the kitchen," or "stick to making babies," we know that these sexist attitudes still prevail.

But as more and more women have entered the workforce, pursued higher education, and delayed or opted out of marriage, women have moved into the public domain that has traditionally been reserved for men. Sexual harassment has become a practice that some men use to maintain their dominant position. The way feminist Barbara Houston sees it, sexual harassment

> ... is a reminder that we are not to consider ourselves equal [to men], participating in public life with our own right to go where we like when we like, to pursue our own projects with a sense of security.[4]

Each incident of sexual harassment is a tacit reminder that women are infringing on male territory. When female students are taunted and teased out of math and science, ridiculed as they walk down the school hallway, and intimidated into silence during class discussions the message is clear: this is not your space.

Of course, not all men sexually harass women. But the problem is so pervasive that we need to look beyond individual males to see what it is about our social structure that allows so many to do so.

Sexual harassment and other forms of violence against women are the logical products of a culture in which women are generally devalued, reviled and mistreated. Despite the gains made by some women over the past century, the continual devaluing of women's work, the lack of women in positions of authority and decision-making, the continual resistance to women having control over their own bodies, the visual representations of women as sexual objects, and the disparaging jokes about blondes, mother-in-laws and bimbos are just some of the ways the diminishment of women remains embedded in our cultural attitudes and practices. Sexual harassers don't just hatch in high school; they have evolved from years of training in a society that conditions them to treat women as less important than men.

The roots of sexual harassment start early, long before girls and boys ever get to school. From birth, there are a myriad of ways children get the message that boys are more valued than girls. In the not too distant past, unwed mothers were pressured into marriage as a way of saving their children from the shame of having "no name." This was a requisite only a man could provide.

Regardless of their employment status, women spend two to three times more hours on housework than their male partners. In his study of working wives and working husbands, James Pleck found that, on average, men's daily contribution to household tasks increased by only two minutes when their female partners were employed.[5] This means that whether or not women are working outside the home, they are shouldering the bulk of the responsibility for keeping the household in order.

Because our society attaches greater value and financial renumeration to activities carried out in the public world, women's greater attachment to the home can limit both their status and economic resources. As a result, women's household responsibilities increase the likelihood that they will be in subordinate positions to their male partners.

When children are raised in a home environment in which women are subservient to men, they are more likely to accept these unequal gender roles. Mary told me that her brother was always cutting her down, claiming that she was "a stupid girl who couldn't do anything." After all, her dad told her mom the same thing. When boys are reared in an environment where females are seen as inferior, is it any wonder they treat girls so destructively outside the home?

HARASSMENT BEYOND THE SCHOOL SETTING: THE VIOLENCE CONTINUUM

Sexual harassment is a part of the continuum of violence that restricts the lives of girls and women. In our society — where 27% of women are sexually assaulted at some point in their lives; where 49.5% of these women are under the age of seventeen at the time of their first assault; where 65.5% of female victims are sexually assaulted by males they know; where 60% of college-age men have reported that under the right circumstances they would use force, rape or both in sexual relations with women; and where the degradation and violation of women through pornography is a billion dollar business — every incident of sexual harassment reminds women of their potential to be abused by men.[6] Before zeroing in on schools, I felt the students needed to develop a broader understanding of the larger picture of violence. Only in this way could they understand the implications of sexual harassment and how it affected their everyday lives.

The young women talked about the harassment and other forms of violence they encountered in their jobs, on the streets, on public transportation and in other settings of their lives. These experiences are closely related to my specific focus on sexual harassment in schools. I think the young women were unable and sometimes unwilling to separate out harassing incidents at school from their broader experiences of abuse. They lived them as connected and, so, they refused to see them as disparate and isolated events.

Women are never sure when harassment will escalate to a more extreme form of abuse. This is why seemingly minor incidents of harassment can feel so threatening. The students I interviewed were often wary of the stares and ogling they received from males. As Beatrice explained, "You never know what might happen next."

The following account of my own personal experience, taken from the journal I kept along with the students, demonstrates the fine line between threatening and non-threatening male behaviour and the ease with which this line can be crossed.

> A man began to walk closely behind me, then finally beside me. He made me uncomfortable and I didn't want to talk to him so I turned to cross the road. He stopped and watched me. When I saw him turn and continue walking, I began to walk up the street again. He was walking very slowly and I knew I would catch up with him at the light, so I slowed down. When I saw the light was green I picked up my pace and crossed the road. He stood on the corner and shouted, "Want to fuck, slut?" He seemed in a rage. I pretended to ignore him but walked quickly into the Board of Education which was two buildings away. He followed me and when I went in the front door, he came right up to the door and started pacing back and forth. He finally left but stood across the road watching the building. When I left the building three hours later, I kept checking behind me as I walked home.

If we really think about it, sexual assault almost always begins with some type of harassment: a threatening comment, a menacing look, an unwanted touch. This is why the concept of a continuum is so important: it helps us to see how the various forms of violence are connected and it gives us a sense of the spectrum of violence in women's lives. By the time young women reach high school, they have usually come to accept male violence as an inescapable part of life and many have already experienced it. Sexual harassment at school is just part of the bigger picture.

Being harassed at work was a common problem. Many students had after-school or summer jobs that provided them with much-needed spending money for things such as clothes and entertainment with friends; some were putting money away for university. Colleen worked in a candy store and was constantly propositioned by male customers in ways she often found revolting: "I'd like to eat your hot lips; the ones with the hair around them." Helen's boss said he wondered "how she'd look in her underwear." During a job interview, Jennifer was asked: "You have a problem [a period] every month. Can you work through it?" She expressed her disapproval of this question and the job was given to someone less qualified.

Being harassed on the street was a routine experience that usually involved a combination of whistles, catcalls, horn-honking and sleazy invitations shouted by both adolescent and adult males who passed by them in cars: "Do you want to have sex?" "Let me suck you between the legs." It wasn't uncommon for the young women to be followed by individual men or groups of men who would verbally intimidate them: "Where do you live?" "Are you a virgin?"

On one of our group meeting days, Beth had been late for school because she had ducked into a variety store to hide from two guys who were following her in a car. When she arrived late for class, she was put in the uncomfortable position of having to explain her tardiness.

Almost all the young women had received obscene phone calls at their homes and for four of the students the calls were so persistent they had been forced to have their phone numbers unlisted. (Throughout this study, when I needed to communicate with them by telephone, I contacted them through a friend.) Although some calls appeared to be random, the caller would often have information that indicated he had specifically targeted a certain girl or a certain *kind* of girl. Minority students, for example, tended to get calls that were blatantly racist. One caller said he had phoned Chen's number because he wanted a Chinese girl to help him "scratch his dick." Ruth, a young Black woman, received a call from a man who said he'd had too many white women and wanted to try something different.

For students in the urban centres, leering and sexual gestures are just some of the harassing incidents that happen on public transit. This includes: "men looking at you, licking their lips"; sexist and racist comments ("I hear Black girls like white guys' dicks"); and flashing and masturbating ("The guy turns around, whips it out [and] starts playing with it"). Even as they waited to board buses and other modes of transportation, these young women often had to contend with crude and demeaning comments and propositions: "I want you to come to my house ... come now girl, give me head."

Tara was really shaken up by the comments made by the coach of a men's rugby team, as she and a friend watched them practice:

> [My friend and I] were at a rugby practice ... my boyfriend was playing ... . The coach was older, he was in his forties and all the players were between eighteen and twenty-five and we were watching them. They were doing their laps around the football field and stuff and they started slacking off. And the coach said, "Come on boys, if you guys do really well and play really hard in this practice, these girls over here will give you all head."

Understandably, Tara didn't attend any more practices and she stopped going to her boyfriend's games.

Although I was focusing on sexual harassment, some young women told me about incidents that were clearly a further step on the continuum of violence: sexual abuse and incest. After her interview, Beatrice explained that focusing on her experiences of sexual harassment had been difficult because what always stood out in her mind was "my grandfather was sexually abusing me." Dora was still afraid to be alone with an older brother who had molested her when she was younger. And Jennifer had never told anyone about the uncle who always wanted her to touch his genitals or the cousin who molested her, because she simply assumed that "there's always one cousin you have to beat off. I think everybody has one."

Harassment is only part of the continuum of violence that females must constantly face. When young women spend so much of their lives looking over their shoulder for fear that a seemingly innocent comment or gesture could be a precursor to a more violent act, then each incident must be seen as a thread in the violent web that contains them.

MORE BARRIERS: RACE AND CLASS

Because the groups were so diverse the young women came to understand how their various economic and cultural backgrounds accounted for the different ways they experienced sexual harassment. "Sexual harassment" is typically perceived to be about gender, as though this aspect of ourselves can be divorced from our other attributes. Certainly, gender is the most salient feature in "sexual" harassment but women are not a homogeneous group. As Jessica put it, "When you think about sexual harassment, you've got to think about people's sex, colour, race."

Many of the young women spoke frankly about the racial slurs that were a prominent feature of so much of harassment they endured. Ruth claimed that most of the verbal hassling she got began with the phrase "I hear Black women are ... " These comments occurred everywhere: at school, on the street, on public transit. Most of the remarks came from older white men.

Lyla said a lot of the Asian girls at her school are new to Canada and so they "don't speak English very well." Other students act as though these girls "don't count for much" and so they don't "stick up for them" when they get harassed.

Because they feel so unsupported these young women are "too scared to stick up for themselves."

The connection between sexual harassment and class hasn't been explored in great detail. But there's no doubt that young women from low-income families have even more limited options for coping with harassing behaviour. For example, some students explained that they tolerated the severe sexual harassment they were suffering in their after-school jobs because they desperately needed the money and they feared they would be fired if they complained.

Students from low income families felt they had no choice but to put up with this harassment. As Izabela explained, "My parents will think 'Oh, why did she quit? We need the money.'" Because they wanted to hold on to their jobs, most of the young women just tried to endure the taunting and teasing they experienced at work.

According to Nan Stein, sexual harassment at school can have grave consequences for the future economic status of all female students:

> Sexual harassment in an educational setting is more than an uncomfortable situation resulting from the trials and tribulations of adult sexuality. Rather it is an experience that interferes with a young woman's access to the education of her choice and therefore seriously threatens her future occupation.[7]

But for young women who are faced with limited financial resources, sexual harassment may be one more factor that discourages them from even pursuing their education.

Undoubtedly, sexual harassment is a problem that limits the educational opportunities of many young women. But the consequences can be even more devastating for those who are also struggling with the additional burden of race and class barriers.

WHY FOCUS ON SCHOOLS?

Young women's experiences of sexual harassment are obviously not limited to schools. But the sexual harassment young women suffer at school sets a precedent for the type of behaviour they expect to face elsewhere. After all, school is the nucleus of their adolescent life: a place of friends and peers; a place of trusted adults; a place where they expect to expand their life opportunities. "If you get treated badly here," Mary Beth told me, "you know you can expect to get the same thing in public." Being harassed at school teaches young women to accept this behaviour as an inevitable part of everyday life.

For many young women, sexual harassment in high school is merely an extension of their elementary school experience. Teri recalled that a typical recess activity of the grade five and six boys was to chase and catch the girls. Once the girls were caught, all the guys "would gang up" on them and touch and grab them; mostly they would "grab everybody's crotch." She also told me about an incident where she had been "flashed at" by a boy in her grade six class, an experience she described as "frightening":

> I was in class. This guy came by the classroom and he stood there at the door in the hallway so that the teacher couldn't see him. He whipped down his pants and stuck out his dick and he started wiggling it and playing with it .... And he said, "C'mon let's go" with his hand.

In one school, the senior boys used rating sheets to record and, then, compare the scores they gave to their female classmates. Even in the primary grades, these students had been labelled as "pigs," "cows" and "sluts" by their male peers. Jennifer remembered being called "a douche bag" by a group of grade two boys.

For Chen, "everything happened in grade eight." She described her male teacher as "perverted" because he was "always looking at the girls and winking at them ... calling them honey." At the end of the year, he celebrated the passage of male students into high school by showing them the pornography in his drawer.

By the time these students hit high school, they were already accustomed to the diminishing behaviour that is part of a long, steady process of intimidation designed to pressure girls into their expected role as subordinates. And, I assume, at the same time, the young men who expressed this behaviour were getting practice at playing out their expected role as dominants.

The behavioural patterns that set the stage for male dominance and female subordination begin early and, when educators fail to intervene, schools become places where these patterns get reinforced. Researchers like Jane Eyre have found that even in elementary schools

> ... assumptions about women as inferior to men, the sexual objectification of women, subordination and domination of women through talk, silencing, limiting access to space and resources through physical violence or the threat of it [are] an everyday occurrence.[8]

Is it any wonder, then, that these high school girls considered sexual harassment an accepted part of their educational experience? As Clare told me, "You just get used to it."

During my fifteen years as an elementary school teacher, I hadn't recognized as sexual harassment the name-calling, skirt-flipping, and bra-snapping behaviour that boys often inflict on girls. Like many educators I had come to perceive this behaviour as part of the natural order of things: "Boys will be boys."

Not that I overlooked disruptive behaviour in my classroom; on the contrary, I considered myself a strong disciplinarian. This meant, however, that much of my attention was directed toward containing disorderly boys so I had less time for female students and less aggressive male students. Perhaps this is why, in looking back, I can barely remember the girls. What has become of them? For years now I've read about girls fading further and further into the background as boys appropriate more and more of the verbal and physical space in schools.[9] Claire made the link between sexual harassment and the erasure of girls in her poignant comment: "When I get sexually harassed, I feel like I don't exist."

The harassment levelled against these young women at school ranged from routine experiences of insults and objectifying comments to periodic threats of rape and murder. Their stories are not unique. The prevalence and severity of their accounts have been corroborated elsewhere. In a study recently conducted with 2,000 female students in the United States, 89% of the girls reported having experienced inappropriate sexual comments, gestures and looks; 83% had been touched, pinched or grabbed; and 40% said that these incidents occurred daily at school.[10] Since the completion of my own research, I have conducted workshops with hundreds of teachers and students who relate experiences that resonate with those of the girls I interviewed.

Considering that sexual harassment is so rampant in our schools, the silence that surrounds this problem is perplexing. Sexual harassment still gets left out of many of the surveys and discussions of violence in schools. In fact, of the ninety-four Ontario School Boards that responded to a survey conducted by Pat Staton in 1992, only 37% indicated they had implemented sexual harassment policies that covered students and 29% had no plans to develop such a policy. Some boards rationalized their decision not to develop a sexual harassment policy for students by claiming that "there have never been any complaints."[11] It was therefore assumed that sexual harassment was not a problem for students.

The young women I interviewed challenge this assumption. Instead, their stories suggest that life for female students is often a grim battle against a hostile and threatening school environment. Educator Carol Shakeshaft sums it up this way:

> If an unfriendly power had attempted to impose on males
> the limiting and harmful education that exists for females
> today we might have all viewed it as an act of war. In ...
> schools today, females are truly a gender at risk.[12]

WHY IS HARASSMENT OVERLOOKED?

One reason that sexual harassment in schools has received so
little attention is the difficulty in disentangling harassing incidents from what we have come to accept as ordinary male-
female interactions. Dealing with this problem requires that
we dig deep and lay bare the sexual politics that underlies
boys' diminishment of girls and acknowledge the ways that
schools have reinforced the very behaviour that maintains
gender inequality.

The way Jacqui Halson sees it, schools help to reproduce
the existing power imbalance between men and women by
failing to recognize the significant impact of sexual harassment on the lives of female students and by failing to intervene. When schools allow such abusive behaviour to continue, Halson believes that young women learn to cope as best
they can with the full knowledge that the disrespect, contempt and violence directed at them by boys and men is considered normal.[13] This means that unless sexual harassment is
acknowledged as a problem, schools will continue to support
those male students and teachers who practise their sexual
domination over young women, while ignoring those young
women who are being coerced into subordination.

Male students' shocking responses to a poetry exercise
assigned by one English teacher are poignant illustrations of
the misogyny that seeps into our schools and breeds a new
generation of abusers. According to these students:

> A woman is: "scum that paints her face," "something to
> kick when you are drunk," "a thing to beat around the

house," "an ugly thing that increases the population," "a moaner," "a slave," "an object of ridicule," and "a thing to use in clearing away the empty beer cans." A man, on the other hand, is "magnificent," "brilliant," "the master of women and the world," "superior," "stylish," "a person who makes the world run," "mature," "inventive" and a "maker of children."[14]

The teacher was understandably surprised and shaken by these comments. I'm sure most of us find these statements disturbing. The underlying message is clear: females are inferior, defective objects; males are superior to them.

Feminist psychologist Jean Baker Miller notes that once a group has been dehumanized in this way it then becomes normal to degrade them and to treat them destructively.[15] This means that ignoring the harassing behaviour that boys inflict on girls is tantamount to handing them a licence to abuse women. In fact, Nan Stein has found that young women telling their stories of sexual harassment at school sound strikingly similar to adult women who have been abused by their male partners:

> I feel very terrible. I felt it was my fault, but it wasn't. I didn't tell teachers or the principal what happened. I think my problem is being scared. I'm scared they're going to do something worse if I tell ... .

> It made me feel cheap, like I was doing something I wasn't aware of to draw this kind of attention to myself. I could never stand up to him because I told him to stop, he'd threaten me, so I began to act like it didn't bother me ... he'd hit me (hard enough to bruise me twice) and then pin my arms behind my back till it hurt and push me against a wall and tell me all the awful things he would do to me if I ever hit him again, so I quit standing up to him again ... [16]

Stein warns that such accounts are powerful indicators that schools "may be training grounds for the insidious cycle of domestic violence."[17]

This is not to deny that boys get harassed too. But when boys are put down they are usually described as being like females or gays: the insult is being called something other than a "real" (that is heterosexual) male. Moreover, boys tell me that these comments are usually expressed by other males and that the impact isn't as great when girls make similar statements. One boy realized that this was due to the lesser social status of females. As he put it, "They're not as high up as we are."

And, ironically, girls who harass boys often jeopardize their own safety. During one interview, a young woman told me she was concerned about a female student who "harassed guys" because she worried that the student's behaviour could give the males licence to abuse her:

> I know one female who harasses guys .... She'll go right up and grab their rear end. She'll say things to them like, "Hi, sexy" or "What are you doing tonight?" A few of the guys have actually come over to her, after she says that. And I'm afraid for her because if she keeps that up she could get in trouble. If the guy comes over and starts talking to her ... he might think she likes him in that kind of way and he might try something she doesn't want him to. It might turn out to be something pretty bad.

Males' harassment of females is perceived as natural or as a threat; females' harassment of males is considered an invitation. This accounts for much of the difference in the way women and men experience sexual harassment.

The harassment of girls must always be considered in light of the ever-present threat of males' violence that restricts their lives. As one student explained, "Some guys might get sexually harassed but they're not in the same boat as we are. We're afraid to walk down the street. We always have to look behind us."

Another reason the sexual harassment of female students has been overlooked is the common perception that sexual harassment is primarily a problem experienced by adult women in the work-place. One student told me she didn't think she could be harassed because she didn't have a full-time job. What hasn't received much attention is the harassment women encounter outside their jobs (for example, on the street) and the experiences of younger women. Because the sexual harassment of women in work-place and academic settings has been well documented, we now understand the damaging effect of this behaviour on adult women.[18] However, we have yet to seriously consider how sexual harassment affects younger females.

A third reason that sexual harassment hasn't been recognized in schools is the censorship that continues to surround this issue. Ironically, while much of the language used to demean women is considered too obscene to be made public, women who object to the use of this language are rebuked for being too sensitive. It is curious, for example, that Anne Dagg and Patricia Thompson weren't permitted to include in their book *MisEducation* examples of the misogynist graffiti they found on desks, walls, and other public areas within the educational setting. The publisher's rationale for this censorship was that "to print such material would be politically *too sensitive.*"[19] An interesting choice of words. Women within those institutions encounter these messages everyday; whose sensitivities are being protected by prohibiting their publication?

In the same vein, a United States newspaper received numerous letters complaining about a story on sexual harassment in which a reporter had included the vulgar language that had been directed at a fifteen-year-old girl by her male classmates. The complaints were about the publication of such offensive language; there was no outrage about the use of this language against the young woman.

In fact, the outrage is more often about the ways the very notion of sexual harassment is harmful to males who must so carefully monitor their behaviour for fear of being falsely accused of harassing women. And still, the voices of girls and women who are continually subjected to this demeaning behaviour remain muted. How do you find the nerve to tell your teacher or your parents that you haven't been attending a particular class because some of the male students keep teasing you about giving them a blow job? One reason young women don't report this behaviour is that they can't bear to repeat it.

EDUCATORS AND SEXUAL HARASSMENT

My intention is not to blame teachers for the sexual harassment that goes on in schools (unless, of course, they participate), but to stress that they need to recognize and confront it. This is no simple request. Like students, many educators aren't informed about sexual harassment; some also experience it themselves.

The young women I interviewed had often witnessed their female teachers being harassed. In one case, a teacher who had given a male student a failing grade because he had not completed the coursework was called a "fucking slut" as the student stomped out of her room. Recently, a British newspaper reported an incident in which a male student cornered a young female teacher, pretended to unbutton his pants and asked if she would "like a taste of what was inside." When she reported the student, the principal dismissed his behaviour as nothing more than a young man's natural reaction to an attractive female.

> He had told [her] the boy was 'girl mad' at the moment. He said she was young and attractive and could expect this sort of thing to happen; only when she got nearer thirty could she look forward to the sexual anonymity enjoyed by the rest of the staff.[20]

If a school administrator can be so glib about a male student sexually threatening a female teacher, how safe are the female students and staff in his school?

In 1980, Anne Whitbread wrote about the appraising remarks, obscenities and physical touching that women teachers had endured from their male students. She explained why this type of behaviour was tolerated within the school.

> Amongst most of our colleagues the subject of sexual harassment was either a joke or an embarrassment. After all, more than a few of them considered it perfectly within their right to pat or pinch female staff at will and if the women were complaining about the boys doing the same, where did this put their behaviour? [21]

The locker-room antics common in many school staffrooms foster a general school climate that is supportive of the hostile, dismissive and demeaning attitudes toward women that promote sexually harassing behaviour. It is perplexing that so many educators fail to see the connection between this behaviour and other forms of abuse. For example, Victor Ross and John Marlowe, school administrators and authors of the book *The Forbidden Apple: Sex in Schools*, claimed they were horrified to have uncovered hundreds of incidents of sexual abuse in schools. Yet they referred to male teachers' and administrators' sleazy and objectifying comments about women as nothing more than "lounge chatter."

> We are begrudgingly tolerant of the lounge chatter about the sexual attributes of a school's girls-women. Most male administrators have either participated in or observed ribald conversations about the sexual allure of some particular female student. No doubt the administrators are happy that parents aren't privy to these exchanges, but nonetheless the conversations are seldom discouraged. Sexist? Probably. So be it. Men talk about women. [22]

According to sexual harassment educators Robert Shoop and Jack Hayhow:

> It is in these kinds of conversations that the seeds of sexual harassment are planted. Locker room humor, sexist jokes, and ribald stories lay the foundation for men to consciously

and subconsciously think of women in only sexual terms, and more specifically, in terms of derision and ridicule.[23]

When administrators such as Ross and Marlowe don't see a problem with male teachers' sexual comments about their female students, it's not surprising that sexual abuse is such a big problem in our schools.

Unfortunately, those in the school community who dare to make an issue out of the sexual antics of males often find themselves dealing with another form of harassment: backlash. One teacher was warned she would never get promoted, if she kept making a big deal about such trivial behaviour. In one school, the male principal stormed out of a staff meeting when a female teacher demanded that he do something about boys who were harassing girls in the school. Some students and teachers have found that the harassment only gets worse when they report it, particularly if school officials don't take the complaint seriously. Many concede that it is better to be silent then to exacerbate the situation by speaking up. This, of course, is what backlash is all about: it is a tacit reminder that our resistance to abuse will be met with further abuse.

But things may be changing. The 1992 *Franklin* v. *Gwinnett County Public Schools* decision in the United States Supreme Court has sent a strong message to school boards that the sexual harassment of students must be taken seriously. In this case, the school had failed to respond effectively to Christine Franklin's complaints about a male teacher who was harassing her.

Since this decision, a number of United States school districts have been found liable for the sexual harassment of students in their schools.[24] The largest settlement to date was paid out by the Chaska, Minnesota school district. In this case, a female high school student charged that school authorities had not responded appropriately to her complaints about the demeaning graffiti, lewd comments and humiliating and degrading acts that she endured at school.

The State agreed. The Chaska High and School District 112 was found to have created "an offensive atmosphere that promotes sexual harassment in general."[25] The student received $40,000.

While there has yet to be a similar ruling in Canada, there is increased likelihood that school boards may face legal liability if they fail to deal effectively with the harassing behaviour to which students are being subjected. While it is unfortunate that it may take such a threat to move school boards to act on this problem, there is some consolation in knowing they can no longer afford to ignore the behaviour that so severely diminishes the educational experience of their female students. As one teacher put it, "It's about time the authorities started looking at what's really involved in achieving equal opportunities."[26]

Chapter Two

GENDER BIAS AND THE STRUGGLE TOWARD EQUAL OPPORTUNITY

FEMALE STUDENTS may be propelled forward by the promise of equal opportunity, but they often run up against a wall of sexual harassment that hurls them back behind their original starting point. Dazed and disoriented they wonder, "What did I do wrong?" The current notion that girls now have the same educational opportunities as boys can be hazardous for female students. It is true that the numbers of girls enrolled in non-traditional areas has risen over the past couple decades, but that doesn't mean these disciplines have become friendly places for them. One young woman told me she didn't like science because she wasn't "any good at it." But when I probed further, she described the anti-female comments she often heard in her class. As she put it, "When you get put down all the time, you end up feeling like you can't do anything."

In 1986, the Massachusetts Department of Education published a curriculum guide entitled *Who's Hurt and Who's Liable: Sexual Harassment in Massachusetts Schools.* Included in the document is the testimony of a young woman who described the "everyday" harassment she and other female students endured in their electronics program:

> One female in diesel shop refused to go to lunch during her last two years of shop because she was the only young woman in the lunchroom at the time. When she went to the cafeteria, she was pinched and slapped on the way in, and had to endure explicit propositions made to her while trying to eat her lunch.

> ...Two female students in automotive shop found it necessary to phone when one was going to be absent because the males in the shop preferred to harass them when there was only one in the shop; this also included subtle pressure for sexual activity from the male shop teachers.[1]

Girls have been pressured to enter male-dominated areas without much consideration about the ways they are treated there. Often they're faced with the dilemma of staying in a hostile environment, or dropping out and dealing with ridicule about their inability to handle the physical or intellectual rigours of "men's" work. This is the kind of situation that has caused educators like Pat Mahony to worry that equal opportunity initiatives may have "made life more, not less, difficult" for female students.[2]

Equality of opportunity means much more than giving girls access to an education that's geared to boys. It means making schools comfortable, supportive and safe places for female students to be. If we really want to provide an equal education for young women, we need to change the focus of our equal opportunity initiatives. As Dale Spender has so eloquently written in her poem "Gender and Marketable Skills: Who Underachieves at Maths and Science":

> ...We can chase our own tails
> And spend years
> Testing girls for their own inadequacies
> We will not find them,

For we are looking in the wrong place.
The underachievement lies not in the girls,
But in those who do not wish to accept them
As equal.[3]

Unless we deal with the ways girls get treated in schools our efforts to provide gender equitable education will be futile. If girls are ever going to get a fair education we need to make "equal opportunity" a more meaningful term.

Despite all our efforts to provide an equal education for female students, schools remain places where young women's opportunities are limited. This situation has continued, in part, because our approach to equal opportunity has been based on the notion that there is "something" about girls and women that gets in the way of their success in education. The thinking goes something like this: If we could just get girls to be more assertive, to hone up on their math skills, to stop fearing success and to quit feeling so badly about themselves (to name a few of their alleged deficiencies), then they might do as well as boys in school.

But, unfortunately, despite all the energy directed towards "fixing" them, many young women are continuing to express a lack of confidence and commitment to their education, even when their academic performance is strong. This leaves many equal opportunity advocates scratching their heads, and those who are skeptical of equal opportunity initiatives reaffirmed in their suspicion that girls just aren't as smart as boys.

Of course, this ignores the fact that girls do better than boys in their early years of schooling, that girls in same-sex schools do better academically and go further in their education than girls in co-ed schools, and that women are entering university in greater numbers than ever. But the precipitous drop in young women's self-esteem as they move through the educational system, as well as the lessening of their career goals, are strong indicators that we need to re-examine how we think about equal opportunity. Trying to "fix" female students while failing to confront the harassment they endure at school leaves a major obstacle to equality firmly intact as young women get shoved forward. Is it any wonder that so many stumble and fall?

The palatability of equal opportunity programs that are centred on individuals' flaws makes sense in the context of a patriarchal society in which certain groups have power over others. Those in the most powerful positions (e.g., men, whites, heterosexuals) become the standard of normality and those who deviate from them (e.g., women, people of colour, gays and lesbians) get assigned to the category of abnormality. Jean Baker Miller argues that once a group is considered abnormal, and hence deficient or inferior, it becomes acceptable to diminish them and to block their efforts towards equality.[4]

Our focus on the alleged "deficiencies" of girls has diverted our attention from the destructive ways they get treated in schools. The onus for girls' and women's lack of success then falls squarely on their own shoulders. If they aren't successful, given all the efforts to remediate them, then it must be their own fault. One frustrated educator put it this way:

> ... It is always women who are seen as needing the help because we have the problems. But the problem is male behavior and when is that going to be tackled ... I'm fed up with first-aid responses .... Yet again, we're left dealing with the effects of the problem while the cause goes untackled.[5]

The concept of the "deficient female" that informs much of our current thinking on equal opportunity has a long history. Although the expression of this victim-blaming concept has changed over time, the message is always the same: Something's wrong with the girls. This is the message relayed in every harassing incident directed at female students and it has been reinforced in our never-ending efforts to "fix" them.

THE HISTORICAL SEARCH
FOR WOMEN'S INNATE "DEFICIENCIES"

The focus on females' "deficiencies" in contemporary programs of equal opportunity is a modern version of the same
old story: man is the measure of all things and women just
don't measure up to men. This thinking has fuelled the historic and unrelenting search for all the ways that women are
different from men and the accompanying theories of
women's inferiority.

Around the turn of the century, scientists began looking
for differences in male and female brains as a way of explain-
ing women's alleged intellectual deficiencies. Initially, the fact
that women had smaller heads than men was considered the
obvious cause of women's cognitive limitations. This theory
was quickly dropped, however, when the ratio of brain weight
to body weight was taken into consideration.[6] Scientists realized that women's brains were proportionately larger than
men's.

Scientists then switched their focus from the *size* of the
brain to search for the location *within* the brain that accounted for females' intellectual failings. When the frontal cortex
was named as the site of the highest mental capacities, many
scientists reported that the frontal lobes of males were larger
and more developed than those of females. But scientists
switched theories again when it was discovered that the frontal
region was actually larger in women's brains than in men's.
Suddenly, the parietal lobes became the seat of intellect:

> The frontal region is not, as has been supposed smaller in
> women, but rather larger relatively ... But the parietal lobe
> is somewhat smaller, [furthermore,] a preponderance of
> the frontal lobe does not imply intellectual superiority ...
> the parietal region is really the more important.[7]

So, rather than abandoning the belief that structural differences in the brain account for the gap in women's and

men's intellectual accomplishments and turning to an examination of social factors, scientists kept searching the brain for any difference that then could be translated into a female deficit.

Even the higher scores of girls on the initial tests of intelligence which Binet constructed around 1910, raised few qualms about females' assumed intellectual inferiority to males. Instead, the test was modified until the female advantage was eliminated. Helen Thompson, who in the early 1900s was one of the first women to receive a PhD at the University of Chicago, commented on the reaction to the higher scores of girls on these tests at a time when researchers were obsessed with "proving" that males were innately more intelligent than females.

> So far as I know, no one has drawn the conclusion that girls have greater native ability than boys. One is tempted to indulge in idle speculation as to whether this admirable restraint from hasty generalization would have been equally marked had the sex findings been reversed! [8]

Ironically, while Thompson stressed the importance of considering social conditions in the interpretation of sex difference research, the impact of her own work was minimized by the social constraints to which she was subjected. After receiving her doctorate with the highest distinction and being appointed the director of psychology at Mt. Holyoke College, Thompson was forced to resign when she announced her engagement to Paul Woolley. Married women were not permitted to remain on faculty.[9] One has to wonder how such limiting factors were taken up by those researchers who kept roaming around the brain to find the "cause" of women's lesser achievements.

Ignoring the obvious barriers to women's educational accomplishments has been a historical pattern. In 1903, James McKeen Catell published a list of 1,000 eminent persons that included only thirty-two women. Rather than examining the social factors that barred women from pursuing activities in which one could acquire eminence (remember Helen Woolley), Catell claimed the lack of eminent women reflected the fact that "women were less likely than men to depart from average levels of ability."[10] The greater variability of males was taken as evidence of their superiority because, according to Darwin's theory, variability was the essence of evolutionary progress. [11]

Leta Stetter Hollingworth, one of the few female researchers of this time, responded to claims about males' greater variability by suggesting that social rather than biological factors accounted for the wider range of male achievements. In commenting on the greater number of eminent men that were used as evidence that males were the more variable and hence, the more progressive sex, Meredith Kimball notes that Hollingworth offered the following alternative explanations:

> Housekeeping and childrearing were fields where achievement and eminence were not possible, not because genius could not be brought to bear on these tasks, especially childrearing, but because society did not bestow eminence upon these tasks. That nearly 100% of most women's energy was taken up with these tasks clearly explained their lack of eminence.[12]

Hollingworth's work offered a critique of biological theories of intelligence that neglected to consider women's limited educational and employment opportunities. However, like Thompson, Hollingworth's personal experience offers some of the strongest evidence for the myriad social factors that held women back. As a student in Columbia University in the early 1900s, Hollingworth studied in an academic environment in which many of her colleagues were not supportive of women's education. Women were not eligible for any of the graduate fellowships, only a small number of tuition scholarships were open to female students, the chairperson of

her department publicly campaigned against higher education for women, and most faculty had never worked with
female colleagues. [13]

The accomplishments of women like Hollingworth and
Thompson, despite all the factors that worked against them,
fly in the face of theories of women's innate intellectual inadequacies. Considering the dizzying speed with which women
have entered university since the external constraints have
been lifted — females now outnumber males in university
entries — we have either to question the validity of these theories or to concede that women have been on an evolutionary
fast-track that may soon render them the more progressive
sex.

The current pressure to provide equal education for
women has generated new theories about females' inherent
intellectual inadequacies. Sex differences in brain organization is presently the most popular biological explanation for
women's cognitive deficits and, currently, the most faddish
cognitive deficit is women's allegedly weaker visual-spatial
ability, a construct which is generally defined as the ability to
mentally rotate objects in three-dimensional space. The theory is that women's brains just aren't wired to handle spatial
tasks and this keeps them from excelling in math, science and
engineering, fields dominated by men. Researchers have barely batted an eye about males' weaker performance on verbal
tasks which is curious when one considers that our highest
ranking officials spend more time talking than they do rotat-
ing three-dimensional objects and that, despite women's
allegedly superior verbal ability, most people in these top
positions are still males.

But even more curious is the flurry of attention given to
sex differences in cognitive tasks when the discrepancy in
female-male scores is so small; in fact, the overlap in males'
and females' scores is usually much greater than the difference between them. On spatial tasks, for example, the average

difference in male-female scores accounts for only 1 to 5 percent of the variance.[14]

Given the small discrepancy in female-male performance on spatial tests, women's low representation in fields such as engineering and math can't simply be brushed off as a consequence of an innate spatial deficiency. Something else must be going on. Earlier in this century, women's so-called biological limitations kept them out of law and medicine; they were considered incapable of handling the rigours of such demanding professions. However, the number of women entering these fields spiralled when the external restrictions barring women were removed. Similarly, the scarcity of women in some areas today probably has more to do with lingering barriers than innate inabilities. When a female student tells me that she's dropping math because the teacher "thinks a girl can't do anything," then we know the notion of the "deficient" female is alive and well in our schools.

GENDER BIAS IN SCHOOLS

Researchers like Myra and David Sadker have shown that gender bias in schools is so prevalent that it's impossible for girls to get an equal education to boys. They claim that female students are being subjected to a terrifying "curriculum of sexist school lessons"[15] that ranges all the way from subtle forms of dismissal and exclusion to blatant acts of harassment and abuse. These are the kinds of barriers we need to eliminate if girls are ever going to get a fair education.

In schools, girls get the message that they are second-class citizens in a variety of ways. This is not always intentional, of course. I was one of those teachers who always believed I treated the sexes equally. But I was jolted into facing my own gender biased practices by a simple exercise conducted by

Craig, a student in my grade five class. After completing a math lesson on bar graphs, I noticed Craig taking notes as I moved on to teach another subject. When I commented on his obvious pre-occupation at the end of the day he proudly handed me the results of his day-long project: a bar graph titled "The Students Ms. Larkin Talks to Most." I was stunned to find that only a couple of girls had made the top ten.

Since that time, I've realized that this kind of gender imbalance is pretty typical in classrooms. After almost two decades of conducting research and observations on gender bias in classrooms, Myra and David Sadker concluded that males are continuing to get the lion's share of teachers' attention. These are the kinds of teacher-student interactions that are giving males an edge in education:

- Male students control classroom conversations.

- Males receive more approval for the intellectual quality of their ideas.

- Male students speak out eight times more than female students and whether the comments are insightful or irrelevant, teachers respond to them.

- When female students speak out, they are more likely to be reminded to raise their hand.

- Males get more help from teachers.

- Males are more likely than females to receive attention in the form of praise, corrections, help or criticism that fosters student achievement.

The Sadkers also found that white males are the most likely group to receive teacher attention; followed by minority males, white females and finally minority females. Black females are also the least likely group to get clear academic feedback from teachers. This means that minority girls are doubly disadvantaged because they get discounted on the basis of their race as well as their gender.[16]

How can teachers be so unaware of the disproportionate attention they give to male students? The focus on boys in classrooms is typical of the kind of expected advantage enjoyed by those who are members of dominant groups. One teacher told me she was shocked by the complaints of some male students and parents when she made a concerted effort to equalize the time, encouragement and praise she gave to female and male students in her class. She was accused of favouring the girls. The boys were just so accustomed to getting the bulk of her attention they felt cheated when she tried to even it out.

But the disadvantage girls face in schools goes well beyond their limited contact with teachers. In 1970, the Royal Commission on the Status of Women reviewed a variety of educational materials and found that the creative and intellectual potential of women was either underplayed or ignored in the school curriculum. If girls and women made it on to the pages of textbooks at all, they were generally portrayed in roles that were less powerful and active than those assigned to males.[17] Over two decades later, according to the recent American Association of University Women (AAUW) report *How Schools Shortchange Girls*, material on women continues to be under-valued and under-represented in schools.[18] In 1992, Myra and David Sadker analyzed the content of fifteen new textbooks and found that the names and pictures of males continue to outnumber those of females. In a 631-page textbook on the history of the world only seven pages related to women.[19]

Without a knowledge of the history and traditions of women, girls are less likely to develop a sense of themselves as significant and constructive members of society. The inclusion of active, powerful, female role models in the school curriculum can raise the self-esteem of female students by providing them with the information and inspiration to challenge the lopsided world view that is presented in an education that is focused primarily on the experiences and accomplishments of men. According to feminist educator Katherine Popaleni:

> Inheriting the knowledge that our foresisters were scientists, philosophers, writers, dissenters, wise women, inventors, community leaders and much, much more would ... cultivate in young women the self-respect, personal dignity and self-identity so crucial to developing their subjectivities as active, self-conscious, self-reliant subjects.[20]

Considering that most teachers themselves are the product of a womanless curriculum, it's not surprising that many continue to teach in the same way. But when a male teacher tells me that women's absence from most history texts is simply a valid reflection of their minimal historical contributions, the harm in such a limited and distorted education is obvious. If girls and women are missing from the pages of school texts, then both males and females learn that it is the experiences and activities of men that matter most.

Aside from the lack of women in the curriculum, what message is relayed to girls by the roles that women hold in their schools? Despite the recent advances made by women in education, men continue to outnumber women in administrative positions. According to Gaskell, McLaren and Novogrodsky, this situation has broad implications.

> Having less power in the schools, women quite accurately do not see themselves as co-managers or decision-makers in schooling. And quite accurately, students, parents and male teachers do not see them that way either.[21]

If female teachers have so little power in their schools, how can schools be empowering places for female students?

There's also evidence that we need a major pedagogical shift if girls are going to get a fair education. In their important book *Women's Ways of Knowing*, Belenky, Clinchy, Goldberger and Tarule point out that many girls and women learn better in an atmosphere of collaboration where space is provided for diverse opinions.[22] But many schools still operate on a model in which students are judged and ranked so that competition rather than cooperation is the norm. The authors argue that tying personal experience to knowledge and fostering discussion rather than lecturing are the kinds of "connected learning" strategies that benefit girls. This makes sense when one considers how detached girls must feel from an education that continues to exclude them.

Male and female students may be sitting in the same classrooms, reading the same textbooks and listening to the same teachers, but this doesn't mean they are getting an equal education. In the words of Adrienne Rich, this is because

> ... [The] content of education itself validates men even as it invalidates women. Its very message is that men have been the shapers and thinkers of the world and that this is only natural.[23]

In a number of subtle and not so subtle ways educators communicate the message that girls are less valuable than boys. These are harsh lessons for female students. But even more pernicious is the mistreatment they receive from some of the very people responsible for their education.

HARASSMENT BY TEACHERS

Considering that females are devalued in school curriculum and classroom practices, it is not surprising that so many boys learn to treat girls with disdain. Male students are by far the most frequent harassers of girls in schools. But this doesn't mean that harassment by male teachers isn't a serious problem. According to the results of a recent survey of 4,200 girls who reported on their most serious incident of harassment at school, 3 percent were harassed by their teachers. In all but one incident the teacher harasser was male.[24] Considering that students were commenting on their *most serious* incident, it's very likely that the general incidence of teacher-student harassment is higher.

These numbers are not to be taken lightly. The misogynist messages of one teacher can be transmitted to hundreds of students over the course of his teaching career. The power and authority held by a teacher means that the damaging effects of their harassing behaviour can have serious and long-term implications.

Izabela described some of the "woman-hating" tirades that drove her out of her science class.

> He was totally against women and everything about them. He called his own wife a bitch, things that were unbelievable. In that class we learned everything that he felt about women and towards women. I learned nothing about science that year.

Such teachers are, hopefully, a rarity. But the consequences of such heinous behaviour can be irrevocable: Izabela told me she didn't like science anymore, and she didn't plan to take it again.

But despite the serious ramifications for students, harassment by teachers has received even less attention than harassment by school peers. One provincial teachers' organization recently undertook the task of surveying students about their experiences of sexual harassment in school. Their study was focused exclusively on student-student harassment. Not asking about teacher-student harassment is a glaring omission. We can't claim to be taking the problem of sexual harassment seriously when the harmful behaviour of school officials is overlooked.

I find it perplexing that some of the same educators who are taking a tough stand on harassment by male students are reluctant to deal with the harassing behaviour of their own colleagues. Perhaps there's a fear that acknowledging the problem of teacher-student harassment will be like opening Pandora's box. Or perhaps there's a feeling of disloyalty toward one's co-workers. There's also the possibility that female teachers are concerned about being branded as troublemakers, or worse yet "feminists," if they snitch on their male peers. And, of course, some female teachers may be experiencing the same harassment as their students. Whatever the reasons, the resistance to dealing with the harassing behaviour of some male teachers is getting in the way of making schools safe and secure places for girls to be.

Let me provide an example. Recently, I was invited to conduct a workshop on sexual harassment with grade nine girls. My session was part of the program for a Gender Issues Day which was put together by the staff and administration of the school. Two female teachers from the planning committee attended the session.

As part of the workshop, I presented the students with scenarios of sexual harassment that had been reported to me by the young women I had interviewed. As we discussed the options available to students who might be harassed in similar ways, a few young women commented on a specific male teacher who was always putting female students down. They asked what they could do about it. We brainstormed for a few minutes about the various strategies they might use and I invited the teachers to offer their suggestions. They didn't respond.

At the end of the session, the female teachers told me they didn't agree with my allowing the students to discuss a situation that involved a real teacher; they would have preferred that I stick to the scenarios on the activity sheet. Now certainly, my intention in student workshops is never to develop a hit list of harassing teachers and students. But it doesn't make sense to invite students to a session on sexual harassment in schools and then ask them to censor their own school experiences. This is another way of silencing girls and it means we're only paying lip-service to the problem.

I'm not suggesting that we become sexual harassment vigilantes, but if students have a serious complaint we must be prepared to deal with it. If teachers are uncomfortable with this responsibility, it may be more appropriate to have someone less intricately connected to the school staff, such as the school nurse or social worker, participate in these sessions.

I've also been told that sexual harassment by teachers isn't a problem anymore, because any teacher who behaves in such an inappropriate way is sure to lose their job. Not so, according to the students I interviewed. The stories that follow are examples of the kinds of teacher-related incidents they had experienced in their schools.

It was amazing how often these students were subjected to the traditional cliché about women belonging "barefoot and pregnant in the kitchen."

> I know this one teacher, and he's very sexist. He makes comments about girls all the time, about the way they dress, or what they shouldn't do, what they should do. Women should be barefoot, pregnant and everything.

Considering the force of the Women's Movement over the past two decades, it is astonishing that such comments are expressed at all. However, when elicited by a teacher who has the power to assess and evaluate you, they can be profoundly abusive and damaging.

Some students told me they tried to avoid teachers who had a reputation for being "too chummy" with girls, but this often meant they didn't get the help they needed with their course work. When Lyla returned to school after a two-week illness, she was warned by a friend not to take up her teacher's offer for extra help after class. She told her, "You've got to be careful with that guy. He likes to get a bit friendly with you." Mary Beth complained about one teacher who was always "telling the girls they were pretty and doing things like touching their hair." One of Teri's teachers had eyes that "would always drift down" when he talked to female students. This made her feel so uncomfortable in class she couldn't concentrate on her work.

> I felt like he was perverted. I just really didn't clue in in that class. He would come up and talk to me and he

would look down at my chest. I won't spend time with
him or talk to him. And if I did have a problem, if I was
stuck on something and he said, "Don't be afraid to come
and talk to [me] about it," I just didn't go.

Zoe was particularly apprehensive about a guidance counsel-
lor who told her she "was pretty" and spent a lot of time
looking at her legs and asking personal questions about her
life outside school. What she had wanted from the coun-
selling session was information on courses for the following
year.

Imagine the impact of the following behaviour on a
female student alone in a classroom with a teacher she has
grown to know and trust.

One thing happened with a teacher. Me and my friends,
we had dinner with him and his wife. We go out, we talk,
I can talk to him. And then one time he says, "Hmmm,
you're looking nice today." He looked me up and down
and says "Why don't you come here?" He showed me
some papers and stuff and started putting his hands on my
bum, squeezing my bum. I said, "Hey, what are you
doing?" He said, "You've got a nice bum ... you've got a
nice ass." I was sitting on the desk like this and he was
behind me. So he went to grab me and he put his hand on
my breast and I said, "Oh my God, what are you doing?" I
trusted him so much and all of a sudden he does this.
Later he was saying to a student, "No, she wouldn't fuck
me, not now because I'm married. But if I were single, she
would probably sleep with me or I would probably get
her."

How confident can a young woman feel at school when she is
abused by the very person she looks to for guidance and support?

Being harassed in non-traditional courses was more likely
to affect young women's academic and career choices than
being harassed in other classes. As they ventured beyond the

boundaries traditionally defined for women, sexual harassment was a reminder that they were intruding on male terrain. For example, Lyla told me that some young women in her school had given up their plans for a career in science because they worried that the kinds of anti-female comments made by their grade ten teacher would only get worse as they went further in their education:

> A lot of the girls take science in grade ten because they want to go into the medical field. Afterwards they don't want to take science anymore. They figure if this is what I'm meeting in high school, what kind of opposition am I going to meet when I get to university or college.

Lyla felt that more young women would enrol in science classes, if they didn't have to worry about being harassed.

A few students had withdrawn from courses rather than put up with the hassling they got in class. Jennifer dropped a course because she resented the demeaning comments the teacher continually made about women.

> We have one really bad teacher here. I won't say his name, but a lot of girls last year dropped his course ... he's a pig. That's the only thing I can think of to call him. He does not think a female can do anything.

Lyla explained why so many female students would adapt such avoidance strategies rather than challenge the sexist comments of male teachers.

> ... A lot of girls are afraid that if they speak out, first of all they get oppressed by the teacher, second of all their marks are in jeopardy. They don't know what to do.

But, there were severe academic repercussions for female students who were continually subjected to such behaviour.

> Well, of course it's going to affect your grades because ... if you're interested in a class you're always getting better grades, that's true. But most of the girls they just want to get by the semester ... as long as they pass the subject, they

don't give a shit anymore about what kind of marks they get.

Being put-down, hassled or assaulted by a teacher can be a crushing experience that adds to a young woman's already deteriorating sense of security and self-worth. But the powerful position of teachers makes it difficult for a student to do much about it. Even the collective action of a group of female students couldn't curb the crude, demeaning and abusive comments of one teacher.

> He was saying that his wife was a bitch, that she couldn't satisfy him. She was thinking about getting ideas about careers and stuff and that he doesn't like that in his woman, that she should be slapped around a little bit. Some of us got really offended by it and we just walked out but he still kept on going. What we heard from those that stayed was that he kept on going as if we didn't walk out at all.

When members of the very group responsible for young women's education can treat them so destructively, we know we're a far cry from giving girls an equal education.

Chapter Three

NAMING THE PROBLEM

SEXUAL HARASSMENT is so commonplace, it is often seen as "normal." Researchers such as Liz Kelly have found that most women have difficulty identifying the ordinary, everyday incidents of sexual harassment because so much of this behaviour is considered to be nothing more than natural expressions of masculinity.[1] This explains why the boundaries of "normal" behaviour for men have come to include behaviour that women experience as degrading, humiliating and threatening and why so many women don't name behaviour as sexual harassment if it isn't an extreme form of physical abuse such as rape.

This limited scope of the use of the term "sexually harassing behaviour" acts to protect men's interests because woman are unable to label much of their abuse and, consequently, men are not held responsible for their abusive behaviour. Liz Kelly explains that the power of the label "sexual harassment" is in "making visible what was invisible, defining as unacceptable what was acceptable and insisting that what was naturalized is problematic."[2] For example, only recently with the development of terms such as "date rape" and "marital rape" has the sexual abuse women experience in their most intimate relationships been acknowledged. These aren't new phenomena; they've only recently been given a name.

Dale Spender has written that names are necessary to make an object, an event or a feeling something real.[3] Names are used as a way of classifying and then filing experiences in our memory. Names are cues that jolt these same events back into our consciousness. This certainly seemed to be the case with the students I interviewed. Once the process began, the telling of one incident triggered the memory of another: "So many things happened to me now that I am talking." This out-pouring of stories came from some of the same young women who had claimed four months earlier: "I've never been sexually harassed." Their thinking changed through the process of linking the term "sexual harassment" to the events of their own lives.

SEXUAL HARASSMENT AS "NORMAL" BEHAVIOUR

The students said there were three reasons they had normalized much of the behaviour they now recognized as sexual harassment: (1) the frequency of the behaviour; (2) the way in which the behaviour was interpreted by others, particularly the male harassers; and (3) the fact that the topic of sexual harassment was seldom, if ever, discussed at school.

In terms of frequency, the young women had come to accept as natural those forms of harassment they experienced on a regular basis. For some, this behaviour was part of the backdrop of their daily school life. Fatima explained it this way:

> You don't think about it really ... because it happens all the time, it happens so often it's just a part of life. How can I explain it? It's like you are walking down the street and someone whistles at you. It's as if it's natural for them to do that and if somebody doesn't do that then something's wrong .... It's like whistles all the time, honks all the time — you don't even pay attention to it. It's part of life.

There was a lot of behaviour that students like Tara, hadn't identified as sexual harassment because "it was just what happened every day at school." Jessica recounted how she had always dismissed the constant hoots and hollers of male students because they occurred so often: "I figured it was just guys being guys."

Males' interpreting their various harassing comments or actions as "a simple joke" or "no big deal" also made it difficult for the young women to identify as harassment behaviour they often experienced as distressing. With no external validation of having been violated, either from the harasser or from those who observed the harassing incident, many students would question their own response and try to take on the perceptions of others. Ruth had often found herself in this situation:

> Before it would bug me but I didn't really show it .... Everyone else was laughing so I tried to laugh. I didn't really know about sexual harassment at all.

In many cases, the students told me that their reactions to various acts contrasted sharply with the perpetrator's assertion that this behaviour was "all in fun." Beth complained that she often experienced such "fun" as humiliating and degrading.

> While practising for a school play I stood up to present the opening scene. I had to ask a guy a question .... He smiled, took my hand, grabbed it hard and he pushed me on top of the table and started going on top of me, saying, "Ohhhhh." People were looking at us. I told him to stop, I tried to push away from him but he only let go when other people in the play said, "What are you doing?" I felt ashamed, embarrassed, and stupid. He was trying to be humorous. "It's just for fun," that's what he told me later when I asked him why he did it.

The third reason that students considered males' harassing behaviour as normal was the school's failure to address the issue of sexual harassment. It followed, then, that many students had no way of naming the abusive behaviour to which they were routinely exposed. The problem was compounded when teachers failed to respond to harassing incidents. For example, one student who complained about male students who continually lifted up her skirt in class was told to return to her seat and stop interrupting the lesson. After that, she stopped wearing skirts to school. Another young woman had to endure a male student putting her book down his pants and making sexual propositions while the teacher looked on. In her words, "What can you do when the person in authority won't do anything about it?"

Because the topic of sexual harassment was a "hush-hush" thing at school, something that "no one really talks about," and because they had no label for the demeaning and degrading behaviour that was part of their school life, the students hadn't complained about these incidents. But as Catherine MacKinnon has written:

> It is not surprising ... that women would not complain of
> an experience for which there has been no name ... the
> unnamed should not be mistaken for the non-existent.
> Silence often speaks of pain and degradation.[4]

In fact, most students claimed that although they hadn't previously labelled certain acts as sexual harassment, this behaviour had always had an impact on them. Their sentiments are summarized in Tanya's comment: "It drove me crazy."

And yet, despite the ubiquity of sexual harassment at school and the anxiety the students experienced as they attempted to weave their way around it, our group meetings were the first place where they had openly discussed, and then labelled, the behaviour that so severely limited their education.

Now, equipped with a language that was rooted in their own experiences, and strengthened by the support they had received from other young women in the group settings, the students could speak out about the harassment that was part of the fabric of their school life.

BROADENING THE DEFINITION
OF SEXUAL HARASSMENT

The journals the girls kept were designed to be a record of incidents the young women considered to be sexual harassment in all parts of their lives. Because they didn't have a specific definition to guide them, the students told me they found the task of recording harassing incidents to be difficult. When I interviewed Jessica, she confessed that she hadn't recorded the more common forms of harassment in her journal because they were "an everyday occurrence" and so she "was less aware of writing them down." In discussing her only recorded incident of sexual harassment, one student told the group:

> I wasn't sure if I should put it down because they [the construction workers] hoot and holler at me every day, when I go to school and when I come home. Finally, one day I got so ticked off I wrote it in my journal.

In reality, this student could have reported ten incidents of sexual harassment by this one group of men. It seems likely that the girls usually under-reported their harassing incidents because they had a tendency to dismiss the routine behaviour.

For most students, it was the testimony of other young women in the group meetings that prompted them to reinterpret incidents that they hadn't formerly considered to be sexual harassment. The group meetings provided a place where these students could develop a common language; one that was grounded in their shared experiences. From here, they could go on to talk about sexual harassment in a way that reflected their personal events. They were becoming more fluent in the language of their own lives through mutual support and understanding.

The students' testimonies, however, did not come easily. Initially, when I asked the young women to talk about their experiences of harassment, most were silent. Dora said, later, that she had been "scared to open up" because, until she attended the meetings, she didn't know "how much it happens to everyone else" and she was worried the other students would make fun of her. Other students didn't speak up because they believed the stereotypes about women provoking sexual harassment. They were afraid they would be blamed if they admitted it had happened to them.

Eventually, a young woman would relay an incident that she thought might be sexual harassment. Her story was often followed by the comment "that happened to me too" and then the stories flowed.

> When they were telling their experiences I was going "yeah, same thing here .... Some of these things I wouldn't have thought of as sexual harassment, and then when somebody says, "Well this happened," you start going over it and analyzing it and realizing it is.

As they shared similar stories, the students began to identify as harassment the behaviour they had previously been unable to separate from their ordinary interactions with males. The shift in their thinking occurred when they had the opportunity to interpret their incidents through a common lens, one that developed from their similar events. Tanya explained it this way:

> This discussion has just totally opened my eyes. I feel like I have been walking around blind while all this stuff was happening around me and I was looking the other way.

Clearly, for Tanya, "all this stuff" was not a new phenomenon. It was only when she began to label it that she tended to notice it more. These young women had not been walking around with their eyes closed, but without the power of a name.

During the course of the group discussions, most students altered their thinking about sexual harassment to include non-physical acts. Like many other students, Jennifer had always thought that sexual harassment was "molesting."

In her words: "I never thought of it as being vocal." In general, the young women expanded the range of behaviour they considered to be sexual harassment. One student put it this way:

> This study made me realize what sexual harassment is. Like a whistle or an obscene phone call. I would have never considered that sexual harassment, but now I do.

When I asked the students in their interviews how they had previously labelled the more frequent forms of verbal harassment, they used terms that included "bugging," "teasing," "flirting" and "annoyances." Helen poignantly stated that she had considered such behaviour "just a fact of life."

When the students broadened the parameters of what they considered to be sexually harassing behaviour, many also rejected the common notion that sexual harassment is a minor form of violence: "I think they're all equal.... One's as bad as the next." Tanya pointed out that sexual harassment and other forms of violence "all stem from the same attitude: you can treat women badly and nobody will do anything." As the young women attempted to sort out which behaviour was and was not sexual harassment, many realized how the various forms of abuse overlap. Often they were unable to separate them: "When someone uses insults and comments to make you feel uncomfortable, it can lead to sexual assault." And unfortunately, as I describe later, some had experienced such an escalation first-hand.

IDENTIFYING HARASSMENT AT SCHOOL

Because sexual harassment isn't unique to schools, many students had a hard time sorting out incidents that happened at school from those they experienced elsewhere, for example, on the streets or in public places. As Teri put it, "Stuff like this happens ... everywhere." For students like Izabela, leers and sexual gestures were so much a part of their day they had difficulty pinning down exactly where each incident occurred.

> It happens ... while you are walking down the street, when you are in the [school hallway], whatever ... not every day, but [at least] every other day.

But there was no doubt that many of these young women were dealing with sexual harassment at school on a regular basis and, as I outline later, they devised all kinds of strategies to avoid it.

> The joking and the touching [happen] every day. Like today I was just standing there and some guy came up and slapped me on the butt. I didn't know who it was.

> Gestures, jokes, grabbing, pinching and stuff like that [happen at school] once or twice a day, two or three times maybe.

Even when they weren't direct targets, sexual harassment was a backdrop of their school day because they often saw other female students being hassled by their male peers.

> Grabbing happens a lot; guys going around grabbing girls' asses .... And pinching too. They pretend that they are going to pinch you in the chest .... I'm not just talking about myself, I'm talking about everybody. You see it about five times a day. Walking down the halls, you see people getting bugged all the time.

Perhaps the constant occurrence of such annoying incidents was one reason the young women often minimized them. In the following scenario, for example, Tara, describes the pervasiveness of such pestering at school, but refers to this behaviour as merely "small" instances, probably because they occur so often.

> *Tara*: There have been a lot of instances, but just really small ones.
>
> *June*: What might a small one be for example?
>
> *Tara*: Someone saying something to you, or looking at you and sticking their tongue out the side of their cheek, that type of deal.

June: Who would do that and where might that happen?

Tara: Oh, at school. Just anybody. Males. Or just grabbing themselves and stuff like that. Or you walk down the hall — this has happened a lot since I got my hair cut — I walk down the hall and someone would grab my head and start shaking it and messing up my hair .... That bothers me 'cause I don't like that. Or I will be standing at my locker and someone will come up and start rubbing against me and I'll be, like get lost.

June: So those are the small things. Do they happen very often?

Tara: Every day.

June: And who would do them?

Tara: The guys.

Although such "small" instances were bothersome, the tendency to dismiss them seemed to express young women's tacit acceptance that a certain amount of sexual taunting was just an inevitable consequence of being female. After all, these young women saw men harassing women on the street all the time and, sometimes, they got hassled too. As Mary explained, "That's life."

HARASSMENT BY OTHER FEMALES

According to the American Association of University Women (AAUW) report, *Hostile Hallways*, female students are most likely to be harassed by their male peers. Among girls who reported being harassed at school 57% had been harassed by a group of males; 18% by a male acting alone; 11% by a mixed group of males and females; and 3% by a group of females.[5] Not surprisingly, results from this study showed that male-female harassment was by far the most common scenario.

I always asked the students to clarify the gender of the harasser, so they understood that I didn't assume that harassment was a behaviour unique to males. Despite this, no students reported being harassed by a female teacher and female student-to-female student harassment consisted primarily of graffiti scrawled on bathroom walls.

Ironically, most of the comments found in the girl's washroom, like those typically found in the boy's washroom, denigrated women. Students like Alison couldn't figure this out.

> They write "bitch." They write a lot of things I'll never understand .... I find it stupid and strange when I see girls writing things like that about other girls. I don't write things like that, but if I did, I'd write them about the guys. Because they do it to us.

Young women's diminishment of other young women could well be expressions of their internalized misogyny; after all they've grown up inculcated with messages that they are innately flawed. Denigrating other young women may just seem so natural, particularly when we consider the sheer volume of sexually demeaning labels for women. In one study, for example, the ratio of sexual terms for men and women was found to be 10:1, with 220 terms characterizing women and only 22 terms characterizing men.[6] The reason that women vilify other women may be the result of the accessibility of degrading language with which to do so. The insults flow easily, if not unconsciously, off our tongues.

Moreover, the pejorative connotations of sexual labels that are connected to women (e.g., slut) in comparison to the more power-oriented interpretations of those sexual terms used to describe men (e.g., stud) result in a sexual language that disarms women at the same time as it empowers men. This was evident in the following exchange between Alison and myself:

> *Alison*: That's another thing I can't stand. People saying things about someone ... you hear a lot of it with girls in this school .... Yesterday, this one girl was going to fight another girl ... someone doesn't like

her so she turned around and she says, "Oh, she's
a slut."

June: What does it mean when a girl's a slut?

Alison: She sleeps around with just about anybody she can.

June: And what is the term for a guy who sleeps around?

Alison: He's a stud. All the guys look up to him. I can't
stand that either. It gets me so mad.

Another issue raised by Alison's comments is the common
tendency for young women to police each other with the
tools of their own oppression. Girls and women calling each
other sluts and whores is as much an act of self-contempt as it
is an act of hostility directed at another female. What is being
expressed is a tacit acceptance of their own sexual regulation
or, at the very least, a reluctant acceptance that such restrictions are part of what it means to be female. It's no wonder
this situation makes young women like Alison "so mad."

What's most unfortunate is the way this anger is often
projected on to other young women. Such lateral hostility is
common when members of subordinate groups feel helpless
to change the conditions that account for their unjust situation. Challenging those who hold the reigns on one's life can
feel threatening and futile. Thus the rage gets vented in safer
ways, often at those in similar powerless positions. In fact,
Lyla claimed that one of the reasons young women in mixed-
groups sometimes participate in the female hassling antics of
males is to protect themselves from similar treatment. As she
put it, "If you become like one of the guys, they're less likely
to do it to you."

Such displaced hostility limits the chances for women to
develop the solidarity they need to rise up against their unfair
circumstances. This means that their subordinate situation is
further entrenched. For these students, coming together in
our group discussions was an important first step to their
becoming a unified force.

LESBOPHOBIA, HOMOPHOBIA AND SEXUAL HARASSMENT

As reported in *Hostile Hallways*, 87 percent of girls and 85 percent of boys claimed they would be "very upset" if they were called gay or lesbian. For boys, no other type of harassment, including physical abuse, provoked such a strong reaction. Boys were more than twice as likely as girls to be targeted in this way and they were more likely than girls to call someone else gay.[7]

Homophobia and lesbophobia seem to go hand-in-hand with sexual harassment. Terms like "faggot" and "lessie" are some of the most common ways boys and girls put each other down. The fear and revulsion around same-sex relationships acts as a convenient distraction from the destructive behaviour that is accepted as part of normal heterosexual interactions.

In working with young people and adults about the issue of sexual harassment, I find there's often much confusion about what behaviour constitutes sexual harassment in mixed-sex interactions. I think it's very telling that we still have such a hard time distinguishing between respectful heterosexual flirtation and abuse. I believe that people are beginning to accept that a major condition of sexual harassment is that the behaviour is *unwanted*; but because women are *supposed* to want sexual attention from men it's assumed that a certain amount of males' sexual bantering is welcomed, unless, of course, a woman is extremely up-tight or lesbian.

On the other hand, young people's feelings about same-sex harassment tend to be much more unequivocal. They are more likely to consider that almost any kind of behaviour that occurs in a same-sex interaction could be sexual harassment. Same-sex sexual attention is still considered so repugnant by most people that almost any behaviour is presumed to be unwanted.

One of the young women I interviewed had been harassed by another female student, a situation that really distressed her.

> She was sending me love songs and she was writing me a card, and then she was calling me and following me home and trying to find out all this stuff out about me. I wouldn't be surprised if she did anything to me.

Chen felt "grossed out" by this behaviour because the mere thought of "something happening between a girl and a girl" was so disturbing to her. But her initial feelings of revulsion quickly changed to fear when a female teacher who observed some of this behavior warned her to "be careful" because the young woman "might be gay." This really frightened Chen because she had "heard so much about lesbians, like they could do something to you." Ironically, no teacher had warned any of the young women about male students who were by far the most common perpetrators of harassment and other forms of abuse at school.

In her important book *Homophobia: A Weapon of Sexism*, Suzanne Pharr notes how lesbophobia operates as a handmaiden to male dominance.

> ... Women feel the necessity to distance themselves from lesbians by asserting how much they like men. Liking men is not the issue. Freedom from dominance and control is the issue.[8]

The threat of being labelled gay or lesbian drives many young women and men into rigid and inherently unequal heterosexual roles in which male power and status is built up by cutting females down, and sexual harassment is one of the primary ways this gets done. Unless we confront the homophobia and lesbophobia that are so prevalent in our schools, we won't make much headway in eliminating the problem of sexual harassment.

The way Suzanne Pharr sees it:

... As long as the word "lesbian" can strike fear in any woman's heart, then work on behalf of women can be stopped; the only successful work against sexism must include work against homophobia [and lesbophobia].[9]

Lesbian baiting is one way of squelching women's resistance to the dominant position of men. In the following chapter, young women offer first-hand accounts of the ways they experience this dominance in their schools.

Chapter Four

SPEAKING OUT

THE TESTIMONIES of these young women portray the grim reality of their high school lives. My intention here is to present the raw versions of the students' experiences with very little editing of their voices. At the same time, however, I don't want to depict them as helpless victims; that is far from the case. Many students developed a variety of ingenious ways to avoid harassing behaviour, but these tactics were not always successful and they required valuable energy that could have been better spent on academic work. But, before I go on to the young women's stories, I want to make some general comments about their experiences and provide a framework for the way I have chosen to present them.

There are several forms of harassment. Verbal taunting was the most frequent way the students were harassed, although physical, visual and racial harassment were also common occurrences. Often, a student would be hassled in a variety of ways in a single incident. Chen, for example, was harassed both physically and verbally as she tried to leave the school at the end of the day.

> This guy in the school ... he either ignores me or he grabs me, and this semester he grabbed me three times .... I say, "Stop it," but he doesn't. I say, "Leave me, I am going home, I am late" and he says, "Oh, come on, we will do it

tonight. Don't you miss me? Don't you want to do it?" I say, "We never did and we won't ... just leave me alone, right." He keeps pulling. He is so tight ... and he just keeps grabbing on to me.

What follows are documentations of the young women experiences of verbal, physical, visual and racial harassment at school. In cases like Chen's, where they were harassed in more than one way, I've categorized their story according to the type of harassment that was most salient in the overall incident. I've sorted the incidents in this way to highlight the wide range of sexually harassing behaviour that goes on in schools and to demonstrate the destructive nature of all forms of sexual harassment. There's a tendency, for example, to assume that verbal harassment is much less serious than harassment that involves physical touching. But, in fact, some of the most disturbing accounts from these young women are those in which they were verbally threatened.

The voices recorded here belong to those we seldom hear: young women. Lyn Brown and Carol Gilligan describe young women's loss of voice as a major wound they suffer in adolescence and I hope to avert some of that damage through this work.[1] The stories that follow, then, are relayed in the authentic words of the students.

VERBAL HARASSMENT

Put-downs by male students were part of the fabric of the young women's school life. The frequent levelling of words like "bitch," "witch broad," "fucking broad," "dumb broad," "douche," "dog," "bimbo," "baby" and "chick" against these students or in relation to women in general usually occurred in the context of allegations that women were inferior to or less capable than men:

> In English class we are talking about women's equality in politics. The guys say that the "chicks" would talk too much; we don't shut up.

Through expressions such as "A woman who makes $40,000 a year is a rich bitch," female students were warned that even the "successful" woman (in the conventional sense) isn't immune to males' verbal degradation. Similarly, comments such as "Women don't play basketball. It's a man's sport" and references to girls being out of their "proper" place at school were ways of reminding young women of their exclusion.

> Last year in my English class, I had three [guys] ... sitting there saying "Oh you should be at home, you're a woman. I'm sure there's laundry to do and you should be at home barefoot and pregnant." They're going on like this and they wrote that in my yearbook .... And then yesterday I was sitting outside my science room waiting for my teacher to come, and two guys from my English class last year...walked by me and one of them says, "Don't you know you should be at home in the kitchen?" And the other one turns and says, "Yeah, I'm sure there's tons of laundry to be done."

The objectification of women's bodies was another strategy used to verbally diminish female students. According to Mary, guys "talking about your body parts in the halls at school" was an ordinary occurrence. The statement "Mick Jagger without lips is like a girl without tits" is just one example of the objectifying remarks made by male students in Beth's class. Terms such as "nice ass," "nice tits" and "sexy legs" were used to evaluate female students or as a way to refer to women generally. Zoe told me that she found it disheartening that guys seemed to relate to her as an object rather than as a human being.

> Male students will come up to me and say the usual. That happens out of school too .... They say "nice ass" or "nice legs," or something like that. They wouldn't say anything like "you have a pretty face" .... They go straight to the body.

Whistling was a common form of verbal harassment that was usually followed up by hoots, hollers or demeaning cat-calls: "I was walking down the hallway when one of the male students started whistling and making rude comments." This didn't seem to bother some of the young women; it happened so often they felt it was "no big deal" and they just tried to tune it out. But students like Dora found it to be one of the most disturbing forms of harassment. In her words, "I'm not a dog!" and she didn't appreciate being treated like one.

At school, demeaning jokes about women happen "all the time: during classes, out of school, at lunchtime." Jokes that demean women are so commonplace, those of us who find them offensive are often considered "humourless." Helen complained that even during her class presentation on the topic of violence against women "the guys were making jokes about women."

Not all sexual joking is female focused. But these students told me that sexual joking at school was generally at the expense of women and that ironically similar comments about men evoked strong protests from male students.

> The jokes are always about the girls ... and never about the guys. And when you tell a guy joke, he'll go mental. He'll turn around and say, "How can you say that?"

It's interesting that comments about males, even the relating of documented statistics about violence by males against females have been so strongly opposed by men as well as by some women. The label "male-basher" has been coined as a way of dismissing and silencing anyone who speaks about males in a critical way. I am not suggesting, of course, that we counteract the degradation of females by imposing the same abuse on males, but I think it is useful for any group — particularly those in positions of power — to reflect on the ways they interact with others and to take responsibility for those actions that are harmful.

A common way for young women to be diminished was through remarks about their assumed participation or interest in sex. Such accounts, whether fabricated or real, empowered young men at the same time as they disempowered young women because of the double standard that condones males' sexual activity and holds females responsible for it. Boys are expected to "ask for it" and "try things" and girls are supposed to say no. When a guy "gets it" he's a hero; when a girl "gives it" she's a slut. So allegations about being sexually active or provocative frequently placed young women in the position of defending their reputations. This task was made more difficult by male students' practice of "telling stories about stuff they've done with girls whether it's true or not."

> Like one of the guys ... he likes to flirt with a lot of the girls. I was talking to my friend yesterday and I was telling her ... how he was touching me [and how] I felt uncomfortable. She was telling me [she] had him in one of [her] other classes .... He turned around and said to [her] ... "I know you want it bad [when] I touch you ... on your shoulder [because] you play with your hair and this and that. I know you want it bad, so why don't you come to my house?"

What was commonly related in many of the harassing comments directed at these young women was the notion that their sexuality was their most significant attribute. Alison was particularly distressed by a male student's suggestion that her relationship with her boyfriend was contingent upon her sexual accessibility.

> I talk about my boyfriend a lot because he seems to be the best thing that has happened yet. In class, this guy starts up and says, "Oh yeah, the only reason you get along with him is because you sleep with him every night."

Responding to sexual propositions is tricky because a young woman's honour is always on the line. One shouldn't sound too eager and hence "loose" or too disgusted and hence "up-tight." Claire explained that this is a dilemma young women constantly face at school because:

> There's always the guys who say, "Why don't we get together tonight? Do you want to go to bed?" ... In the halls they come up to you.

Such sleazy comments are ways with which some males tease young women and they aren't always meant to be taken seriously. But, regardless of the intention, the young women were always left searching for a response that would keep their reputation intact.

It wasn't until I had the opportunity to work with these young women that I learned that "rating" female students was such a routine practice. However, as I do more and more work with students, I realize that "rating hallways" are pretty common in schools, and that many girls avoid them. One educator said this didn't surprise her at all. She had watched women being paraded before judges in beauty pageants for years, all striving for a perfect score: that illusive "ten." Why wouldn't boys in schools rate girls on a similar scale?

The standard rating comments ranged from low scores of one or two for girls who were "real dogs" to scores of nine or ten for those who were judged to have "great bodies." Tara described a rating scenario in which male students had developed scoring cards so that the girls' marks were publicly displayed.

> It was hot out. We had just finished playing ball. We came in and we were soaking wet and there was a line of guys down in the locker bay and they all had these numbers and when you'd walk by they'd hold up a number for you, like you were a three or a ten or whatever, but they never said anything. They just held up the number and put it down and when the next girl walked by they'd hold up the number and put it down.

Such scrutiny was anxiety provoking for many young women, because they feared the humiliation of a low score. Being labelled a "two" by a group of young men as other students milled about the halls was a form of public diminishing that shook many young women's already precarious sense of self.

> I don't have very much self-confidence in myself. And it's even worse when a guy is rating you. Because if you get a low number you feel bad.

One student who dared to challenge a male student about this "sexist" practice suffered the ultimate public insult: a score of zero.

> On the first floor hallway I was sitting on the bench, talking with friends. Suddenly one of the guys jumps up and runs down the hallway. When he returns he has construction paper with large black numbers written all over them from one to ten. So the guys went on with their sick way of having fun by rating girls as they passed by in the hallway. I told one guy that he was sexist and by rating young women as they passed by in the hallway he was making them feel very self-conscious and very uncomfortable. I told him he was rude. He said, "Just for saying that, I give you a zero."

Comments about one's clothing and personal appearance are not always sexual harassment. Generally, the incidents the students perceived as harassing were those they experienced as depersonalizing, demeaning or threatening. Being referred to by some physical attribute as opposed to their own name, such as, "Whoa, look at that blonde," stripped young women of their personal integrity by emphasizing their appearance over their personhood.

Because women's value in our society is often tied to males' approval of their personal appearance, some students felt flattered at the same time as they felt threatened by males' comments about their body or their dress. This conflict seemed to stem from their concern that what they perceived as a compliment might, in fact, be a lead-in to demeaning or threatening behaviour. This was the case for Alison whose excitement at being noticed by some of the senior male students in her school was squashed by the crude sexual propositions that followed their initial remarks.

> In grade nine, I was wearing a short mini-skirt and I was walking down the hall and there were two guys down at the end of the hall. And they started whistling. So one guy yelled out, "Hey you, you in the black skirt." They kept bugging me. I finally turned around and said, "What do you want?" They said, "You got legs that just don't quit." It made me feel good but it made me feel scared ... I was afraid they would keep this up. And they did ... The one brother said to my friend, "Tell her I want to sleep with her." And I said to my friend, "I'm not sleeping with him." The next day my friend came back to me and said, "Because you won't sleep with him, he wants you to give him a blow-job."

Women are often leery of male compliments because they are suspicious of the inherent message or agenda behind them. This doesn't mean that males should stop complimenting females. By definition, a compliment is given to make a person feel good about themselves and, in a society in which females are so devalued, women need to be constantly reminded of their self-worth. But when women are valued only for the ways they appeal to men, as was often the case with these girls, they become objects that are used to inflate male egos and their own identities are sacrificed.

The following accounts are particularly disturbing because they describe situations in which young women were verbally threatened by their male peers. One incident involved a phone-call made to the vice-principal at Dora's school.

> This guy called up the school .... He called my house first and said, "I went to school with her a year ago ..." and my mother said, "Well, she's not home, she's in school." Then he called the school and he talked to the vice-principal and

said, "Tell her that I'm going to rape her, you know, I'm going to kill her ...." After that one phone call, the vice-principal thought that I would be better off and have better protection if someone was with me all the time. So I was in all my classes and I had this undercover cop sitting at the back of my shoulder.

When I interviewed Dora a year later, she was still receiving harassing calls at home and she was afraid to leave the house at night. She had no idea who was making the calls and her daily life was one of constant vigilance.

Tara was threatened by a male student who had spread stories about her being the kind of girl that would "do anything you want as long as you pay her." Later, when she met him at a school party he became more abusive and Tara tried to fight back.

I was sitting on my friend's lap and a guy comes in; the same person at the school dance who said, "She'll do anything you want." I was sitting there, and he comes over and he's got a mouth full of beer and he spits on me. I got real mad and I grabbed a beer out of my friend's hand and I started shaking it up and I was going to spray it on him. He said, "If you spray that on me, I'll rape you."

Jessica received threatening phone-calls from at least three male students after she had terminated her relationships with them.

... After I broke up with them I'd get obscene phone calls. They'd say, "Oh you bitch, you better watch out. I know who you are. I know where you live. I know your phone number ...." They'd say other things, get their friends to call. They'd say, "You're going to die; you're a bitch."

When she confronted them, the young men admitted they had made the calls. Jessica explained their behaviour.

I dumped the guy before the guy dumped me. They didn't like that because I was in control. So because of that they were angry. They were jealous, especially if I was going out with someone else.

Because of these phone calls, she now refuses to date males from her school.

And Beth experienced the following incident in class.

> I was talking to a guy who sits behind me. I did not insult him when I was talking to him but he said a sentence and ended calling me "a bonehead." I then said, "You're the one who's a boner." He said "You better shut up before I stick my dick up your ass so hard you won't be able to breathe."

Most people flinch when I read this last account in talks or workshops, and that is exactly why I always include it. Part of my political commitment in this work is to make public the raw material of young women's lives; to provide a forum for the unabridged versions of their stories that are often edited to make the words much gentler on our ears. When a young woman's warning that some guy may "stick his dick up [her] ass" gets translated as a "rude comment," we lose the impact. If we cringe when we hear such horrific words, we are more apt to understand their devastating impact on a fifteen-year-old girl.

Here I have highlighted the litany of ways these young women were verbally harassed. But, in many cases, such demeaning comments are a backdrop to the physically harassing behaviour that follows.

PHYSICAL HARASSMENT

Grabbing was the most common way these young women were physically pestered at school and it was a big part of the hallway hassling with which they had to contend. Tara observed guys "grabbing girls' asses ... two or three times a day" and Claire said for her it was a daily ritual. Even as she headed to one of our sessions on sexual harassment, Amelia complained that she "got [her] ass grabbed."

At the same time as they were being grabbed, many of the

students were fondled by male students in ways that also involved various forms of touching and rubbing.

> They were hugging me and they were grabbing my shoulders and they were touching my hips ... They were touching me and holding me real tight.

For Tara, the following lunch hour scene was typical.

> I will be standing at my locker and someone will come up and start rubbing against me or the guys will walk out and they'll try to touch your chest.

In one class, the persistent rubbing and poking by a male student was both annoying and distracting for Alison, even though she gave the illusion of ignoring it.

> This guy in my class kept rubbing my back and my sides and poking me in the rear end .... At first when he started doing this — he did it for over a month — I just kind of blew it off, like he'll stop if I don't pay attention to it. .... He never did. A few people had to tell him, "Look stay away from her. You shouldn't be doing that." It was a real pain.

In a few cases, young women were pushed, kicked and slapped by male students. When guys went around "slapping girls' asses," the intent was often to be playful (although the young women often found it intrusive). But Mary recalled a particularly disturbing incident in which "a guy held a girl up to a locker and made her stay there while he kicked her." For a three-week period, Beatrice endured a series of kicks and pushes by a male student, because she thought he might let up on her if she ignored him. This was not to be the case.

> The pushing and kicking happened with a guy at school for three weeks. When he saw me he couldn't come up and say hi. He had to push me or, if I was walking, he had to kick me. If he was by my locker, he would just come up and kick me in the ass. It got really serious when I was walking down the hallway in school. He came behind me and choked me. I turned around and I said, "What the fuck are you doing, man?"

It wasn't uncommon for the young women to be followed around the school by male students and, in some cases, to be followed home. I asked the students if it weren't possible that similar schedules, courses and activities might make it likely that some males and females would keep running into each other at school. Some agreed. But Izabela was convinced that the ubiquitous presence of a particular male student throughout her school day was not merely coincidental.

Izabela: I had this one guy follow me ... I felt very uncomfortable because everywhere I looked there was this guy just looking at me ... like from the library to the second floor. Everywhere I turned he would be in front of me.

June: How do you know he was following you and not just happening to be in the same place as you were?

Izabela: Well, I don't think a coincidence happens that much. At first I thought, "Oh my God, he is here." Then in a while I go, "Wow."

June: Did you ever find out who he was?

Izabela: Yeah, through one of my friends. Apparently he was asking her questions about me. I don't know if he was just curious about who I was or what.

It was the young women's concern about the reasons they were being followed that made many of these incidents so disturbing.

I've been followed around the school by a guy. I knew him as a friend but he just kept following me. So I said, "What are you following me for?" He said, "Just to see what classes you have." It got me thinking, "What does this guy want from me?"

In some cases, the young women were eventually trapped or physically restrained by male students who, after surveying them for a period of time, cornered the young women and demanded their attention.

... And then I told you about when I was walking down the ramp near the gym and he wouldn't let me go. He covered me this way, covered me that way and I said, "OK, let me go now." And he finally let me go and said, "Be that way."

Alison was followed around by a male student she had previously dated. In fact, she had ended the relationship because of this behaviour,

I had this boyfriend. He'd follow me around like a lost puppydog. He'd always be there grabbing my arms and saying, "I can't wait until tonight, we'll go to my place." ...This is why we split up. It's almost a year now, and he's still saying things like that. And then yesterday, I was just sitting there and he turned around and looked at me and said, "Do you want to make hot passionate love?" And I said, "Look, please don't bug me." He's still following me around.

The most extreme way the young women were physically harassed was through acts that occurred less frequently than the more routine forms of harassment (for example, objectifying comments, leers and grabbing), but bordered on sexual assault. The point at which physical acts such as touching and rubbing become sexual assault is not clear. Distinguishing between sexual harassment and sexual assault is a difficult, if not impossible, task.

Sexual assault differs from sexual harassment in that the former always involves physical contact. However, in many cases sexual assault is an extreme expression of the various forms of harassing acts. For example, one young woman described the following incident in which the harassment experienced by another female student escalated to more extreme and terrorizing behaviour.

Like she knew these guys ... what happened was they were Black and she was white and one of the guys asked her out and she was in the process of going steady with a guy so she says no. So the Black guy took it as she doesn't want to go out with me because I'm Black. So [he] and a whole bunch of his friends were teasing her for a few weeks and then what happened was she was walking at lunch-time by herself, just going through the parking lot .... And they came up to her ... and she even knew some of the guys. They were still her friends so she didn't think much of it, but they followed her and started fondling her and everything and eventually she was screaming.

Overall, the physical forms of sexual harassment directed at these young women gave force to the verbally harassing behaviour they experienced so often and intensified their vigilance over the behaviour of males. In the same way, these acts warned young women that the demeaning and threatening images and gestures they encountered were not to be taken lightly.

VISUAL HARASSMENT

Leering was the form of visual harassment the students experienced most often. A leer is a form of invasive watching, a look that continues for a length of time and is experienced by the recipient as intimidating or intrusive. As Hilary Searles-Iversen so succinctly puts it, "A leer is a wrong kind of interested look."[2] Joan explained why she found the intrusive stares of male students so bothersome.

It's the way people look at you sometimes. People will look at me and I won't know what they're thinking. They'll have a strange look on their face; it's almost a smile, but almost like an evil look. Sometimes they make me uncomfortable because I don't know why they are looking at me in that way .... It's almost like a perverted thing in their eyes. It kind of worries me ... what they might be thinking.

It was a feeling of apprehensiveness that the young women seemed to use as a criterion for differentiating between a leer and a look. So when I asked Chen to respond to the common accusation that this whole business of sexual harassment has gone too far, because now guys are afraid to even look at a girl, she told me:

> It all depends on how you look at them. You can look at them ... the way you and I are looking, just eye to eye contact. The way somebody will look at you dreamy-like, you wonder what is going through their mind. Or when someone is just staring at your body ... you feel like he or she is going to attack you or something.

Males' gawking seems to signify girls' passage into womanhood. In her article "Growing Up in a Sexual Jungle," Marian Botsford Fraser writes that:

> At some point in their physical development, all female children lose the protection of baby fat and barrettes and become prey in a game in which there are rules only if the law is broken. It is pretty much open season on their self-confidence and aspirations and propriety.[3]

And, she goes on to say that

> ... The worst messages come from men. I have watched the way that grown men feel free to look at young girls. A fat white-haired man wheezing and sweating on a bench in a mall lets his eyes slide all over the body of a pretty teenage girl walking by. A man on the street grunts when he encounters two teenagers young enough to be his daughters. A business man in his fifties mutters, "check out the hot blonde" to his buddy; the hot blonde is not yet 16 ...[4]

Such ogling can crush young women's excitement about their developing bodies, as they quickly learn the risks that accompany their physical maturation. Often, leering is a process used by males to select those females who will be the target of their further sexualized comments and behaviour. So women watch men watching them and are wary of what may happen next.

For Izabela and other young women, being surveyed by males:

> ... happens while you are walking down the street, when you are in the hallway .... maybe not every day, but every other day ... They look at you from head to toe and just make comments and stay very close to you.

Even when they weren't the target of male students' ogling, the young men's public sharing of the ways they scrutinized young women reminded female students that they were never beyond the daunting and judging of males' gaze.

> In one class ... some guys were sitting there and they were just talking. I was sitting beside them and I overhead them. One guy was talking about his friend and he was saying, "Joe has a laugh in gym class. They have pool right now and he wears goggles. He goes under water and he watches the girls' pussies under water."

Sexual gesturing was used by male students to embarrass or intimidate young women. According to Alison, sometimes, when guys don't like what girls are saying "they'll grab themselves or they'll pretend they're jerking off." Beatrice told me the following incident occurred when she was playing soccer for the school team.

> I was in the middle of a soccer game, and someone called me from the stands. I looked over and this guy in the stands grabbed his crotch with his hands and moved it in the up-and-down motion.

She didn't know the student, even though he had called her by name, and she found it difficult to concentrate for the rest of the game because she was worried about being singled out in this way. What if he tried to follow her home?

Much of the demeaning graffiti about males and females was written on bathroom walls and, as I mentioned earlier, the messages in the girls' washroom usually denigrated other female students. These young women speculated that most of the graffiti in the boys' washroom was also about girls, and many worried their name would end up there. Beth uncovered some very disturbing graffiti in her art classroom.

> While waiting for my teacher ... I happened to just wander around the room looking at the art posted up on the wall. I came across a stack of boards piled in the corner with graffiti written all over them. I expected to read "P & I" or "10% true love" or people writing about their favourite bands ... But as I looked at the third board down reading the graffiti, I saw a picture of a naked woman (no arms, head, calves or knees) with her legs wide open showing her vagina, anal opening and breasts. I was shocked to see such explicit graffiti in my favourite class, art. I never thought anyone in our school could draw such violent pictures of women. To me, that picture says mutilating is OK, sexual assault is OK, rape is OK, and that is what I'm scared of the most.

Beth's reaction to this image reflects her awareness of the inextricable link between the various forms of violence; a connection that keeps women constantly on guard.

In some cases, the young women were teased with pornographic images: "Hey, how'd you like a body like this?" One student told me she was relieved when her principal banned pornographic pin-ups from school lockers. Teri was hoping her school would adopt the same rule.

> My friend has a picture in his locker of this naked woman. And when I look I can see it, too. That's disgusting because she's sitting there like this with her legs open .... What a picture. That's sickening because you go to your locker, and that's the first thing I have to see in the morning ... a naked woman.

But degrading images of women weren't always stashed away in school lockers or surreptitiously revealed when teachers were looking the other way. In some cases, they became part of the school curriculum and were publicly displayed. Beth's reaction to her teacher's acceptance of such images in class projects and his tolerance of male students' responses to them is heartwrenching for anyone who has any concern about the well-being of girls in school.

> On the day our advertisements were due, two people had advertisements for coke and swimsuits, both showing women in a very sexual manner. When they were put up guys whistled, hollered, and said, "Yaaa" and "Ohhh." Some guys stood up and clapped. In the pictures both women were lying down, practically wearing nothing and both had their faces not showing or parts of their bodies were cut off .... I looked at the teacher putting up these advertisements. Then I looked at the young women in the classroom. Then I thought of me. I said to myself, "How does the teacher view me?"

RACIAL HARASSMENT

When race is a factor, the experience of sexual harassment can be qualitatively different. For example, while all young women were vulnerable to ratings by males, Black students generally got lower scores than white students.

> The guys would play this game. They would all have ... a number and [they would score] girls who passed by them in the hallway. If it was a pretty girl they'd say, "Ten, right on, you've got her!" If a Black girl walked by they'd go, "Oh my God, she's got such a big ass ...." They'd give her a low score.

The myths and images of women of colour are often communicated through sexual harassment. Much of the verbal harassment inflicted on female students of colour was laced with racist slurs and stereotypes. When a male student told Ruth, "I hear Black girls are good in bed," he was expressing the stereotype of the highly sexed and promiscuous Black woman. Comments such as "I hear Black girls like white guys' dicks" resonated with the common pornographic image of Black women as willing slaves to their white masters.

The message generally transmitted to young minority women, like Chen, was that their race or colour would render them more pleasing or unique sexual partners than white girls.

> ... They were bugging me and they were grabbing my shoulders. They were touching my hips ... and he's saying, "When are we going to get together because I've never made love to a Chinese woman before? I wonder how it feels."

There's a tendency to attribute the harassing behaviour of some males to differences in cultural views of women. But this is just one more way to excuse sexist abusive behaviour. Izabela told me about one teacher who continually made disparaging remarks about women in class. The teacher was Muslim, as was Izabela. When students took issue with his comments, he dismissed their complaints by saying that this was a normal way to speak about women in "his culture." When Izabela told her father that her teacher claimed that putting down women was standard behaviour for Muslim men, her father was enraged. He met with the teacher the next day to express his anger about his culture being used as an excuse for the teacher's sexist and demeaning comments.

The experience of sexual harassment for women of colour is often compounded by other issues, such as economics. More women of colour than white women are in low-income groups and, for this reason, their options for dealing with sexual harassment may be limited. The fact that, following reports of sexual harassment, fewer women of colour than white women leave their jobs may well be a testament to the tenacity and confidence of Black women, but it may also be a reflection of their inability to exercise this option because of their impoverished economic situation.[5]

In schools, there is little support for any young woman who is the target of sexual harassment at school. Young minority women are particularly disadvantaged because they are less likely than white girls to be defended by other students.

I think for [the guys] it's a power trip ... They get to tease some girl, especially a minority girl ... and nobody's going to say anything. First of all, if it's a girl a lot of guys won't say anything, and a lot of the girls won't say anything. You get the minority in there, and *definitely* nobody's going to say anything.

Putting up with the everyday harassment at school can be taxing for any student. But having to deal with racism as well can add to this already wearing task.

For these young women, and for many of those with whom I have worked as a follow-up to this study, verbal, physical, visual and racial forms of sexual harassment are an inherent part of their school experiences. But, certainly as Pat Mahony reminds us, school constitutes only "one site where male sexual violence is learned and practised."[6] These incidents are only part of the larger web of sexism and violence in which young women are entangled.[7] For these young women, the hostility they faced at school infiltrated all aspects of their lives and was played out in ways that both mirrored and extended their incidents of school harassment. As young women move in and out of the various settings of their lives, they come up against a network of abusive incidents that, when taken together, construct a tightly woven web that keeps them stuck in their subordinate place.

THE ULTIMATE HARASSMENT: DATE RAPE

The assumed "entitlement" of many males to intrude on females in a physical way stretches all the way from patronizing pats to mutilating blows and, for this reason, women must be cautious of every physical intrusion and consider what response best guarantees their personal safety. The possibility that annoying pats, slaps and rubs could escalate to such an extreme form of physical abuse is a worry for many

young women who have been physically abused in their intimate heterosexual relationships or know other young women
who have been.

Barrie Levy in her important book *Dating Violence: Young
Women in Danger* notes that young woman between the ages
of fourteen and seventeen account for 38 percent of those
women who report having experienced date rape.[8] Sexual
harassment and date rape stem from the same attitudes; both
are a reflection of men's assumed right to control women in
the public and private spheres respectively. These attitudes are
held by females as well as males. In a survey of 1,700 students
in grades six to nine, 65% of the boys and 57% of the girls
agreed that it was acceptable for a man to force a woman to
have sex if they had been dating for more than six months;
and 51% of the boys and 41% of the girls agreed that a man
had a right to force a woman to kiss him if he had spent more
than $10 on her.[9] Twenty-seven percent of the young women
in a study by Miller and Marshall said they had engaged in
unwanted sex because of psychological pressure from their
boyfriends.[10] They didn't identify these experiences as rape,
but as just part of "what happens on dates."

Because there is so much tolerance for sexual assault
when it is associated with dating, most adolescent girls don't
know when a rape has occurred.[11] Mary wasn't familiar with
the term "date rape," but she had learned through our group
discussions that sexual harassment was a way males could be
abusive to females. So, when her boyfriend raped her, she
claimed he sexually harassed her because she had no other
way of naming her experience.

> During the March Break, my ex-boyfriend gave me a call
> and wanted to talk to me about "things" in our relation-
> ship .... When I arrived everything went smooth, but then
> there came a point when he was being aggressive. At that
> point, I was struggling for him to let go of me. When this
> occurred, he lifted me up and carried me to the basement

and I guess you can say he sexually harassed me .... When I told my best friend she said it was date rape .... I said "no" to him and he still forced his way inside of me.

The way Teri sees it:

... Like girls at school. I'm sure everybody gets whistled at, called at or sometime almost forced to have sex.

In a culture that tolerates sexual violence against women, girls like Teri come to see acts such as sexual harassment and date rape as nothing more than a normal part of being female.

WHY GUYS HARASS

In the end, these students rejected the common notion that sexual harassment was a natural expression of male behaviour elicited by a provocative woman. This theory didn't fit the stories that were shared in our group discussions; most of the students found the sexual antics of males disturbing and they developed all kinds of strategies to avoid them (see Chapter Five). Instead, the young women were more likely to think about sexual harassment as a kind of male posturing, something guys did as a way of gaining status by showing off in front of their friends.

The harassment seemed to be more about the young men jockeying for position within their own group than it was a real expression of their contempt for the young women. It seemed that the way to gain status as a male (and perhaps avoid being harassed yourself) was to participate in female-hassling rituals. This was confusing for the young women who found that some young men were friendly and considerate as individuals, but often resorted to abusive and demeaning behaviour when they were with other male students.

They're fine by themselves. If you talk to just one of them, it's OK. But when they get into groups, they have this ego trip going and put everyone else down.

When guys get together in a group they're a lot braver, because they are always trying to impress. I've known a lot of guys who are really nice when they're by themselves. But as soon as they get in a group you have to watch what you say with them.

Wise and Stanley suggest that one of the chief sources of male power must be the feeling that "half the human race ... are by nature inferior,"[12] and that is why, regardless of their general position within the hierarchy of male students, young men can always assert their dominance over young women. Growing up as a young man in today's society is certainly not without its hardships, particularly for those males who don't have race and class privilege. But as males pass through adolescence, their self-esteem doesn't plummet to the same degree as does the self-esteem of females.[13] One reason for this gender-difference may be that young men come to realize, as Tanya suggested, that girls and women are always considered "less than them." In fact, Tara explained that "treating girls really badly" is one way marginalized male students get to be part of the "in-crowd."

> He just recently moved here and he was having troubles when he first got here, fitting in and stuff. And now that he's with the in-crowd, he'll go to any length he can to get the attention that he wants no matter who he hurts on the way.

Sexual harassment may be more about males' insecurity than anything else, and the current trend is to interpret it that way. But this misses the point. I am not unsympathetic to the difficulties that young men face in their everyday life. The period of adolescence can be a trying time for males as well as females, but we need to question why young women are considered to be the legitimate recipient of the beligerence caused by males' frustrations. Acquiring status and security by beating someone else down is the essence of a hierarchical society and such dehumanization fuels the violence that maintains it. The guys who harass girls at school may be insecure, but their indifference to the impact of their actions on female students suggests a total disregard for the young women as human beings. This is the troubling issue.

The reasons guys sexually harass young women probably vary. These students felt that some male students and teachers used sexual harassment to protect (as opposed to express) their power over women. The impending threat to men of women's increased power was a concern that bonded one teacher to his male students.

> Once I had a teacher say, "Guys we've got to stick together, because if we are not careful the girls are going to rule the world, and we don't want that." He was speaking directly to the males as if the females weren't in the room.

Helen said that, at a time when women were beginning to make large strides forward, sexual harassment was a way men could keep "that little edge over women ... psychologically."

The students believed that the practice of sexual harassment was perpetuated and reinforced by a two-prong process that involved gender socialization and sexual double standards. According to Beth, guys were bombarded with images of women as sexual objects and so, inevitably, they related to women only in a sexual way.

> I feel guys will always be caught up in a world not knowing anything much about women except for great body parts and sex. As long as the media and the language we use in our society keeps feeding them these images, we will never break away from attitudes like this. They think it's good to be "macho" and so they think with what's between their legs and not with what's up there in their brains.

The young women were angered by the double standard of sexual behaviour that gives males sexual freedom, but prohibits almost any sexual activity by females. Although they didn't strictly adhere to this code, most felt they would suffer severe consequences if they ignored it completely.

I hate to say this but guys don't come off looking like sluts. Guys grab girls and they go and laugh it off. It's like they are saying, "I like it, I want it, give me more." And if a guy says it, it is natural .... Well, not for a girl. If a girl does it, then she is just going to get herself in trouble. It drives me crazy.

Guys can sexualize their interactions with young women because the dual code of sexual ethics gives them permission to do so.

Seeing socialization and double standards as the root cause of males' harassing behaviour and having these notions supported by other young women in the group meetings may have been the reasons the female students were seldom victim-blaming when they tried to figure out why guys behaved in this way. In most cases, they took no responsibility for males' harassing behaviour. This was certainly a positive step in the process.

But this perspective also diminished the responsibility of those males who elected to treat these young women in abusive ways. The fact that all males don't engage in sexually harassing behaviour, despite their similar exposure to the socialization patterns and double standards, suggests that some make a conscious choice to harass women. As Mary Beth put it, "Guys sexually harass females because they can." This is what we need to change.

Chapter Five

THE EFFECTS

ACCORDING TO Sue Wise and Liz Stanley, sexual harassment "wears women down by always sounding in our consciousness so that we can never get away from [it]."[1] Jennifer was "constantly aware of it," and Tara said that it's "always in the back of your mind, that somebody's judging you." Indeed, for these young women, sexual harassment was a strong and persistent presence in their school lives.

The overall effect of sexual harassment at school was to create a threatening environment for female students. As Lyla put it, "A lot of girls don't feel very secure at school." In fact the young women's most common reaction to harassing incidents was fear: "You get scared in school. After a certain while you get really scared about all the situations." They worried that even minor incidents of sexual harassment could escalate to something more serious.

> Just what could happen from a wink or when somebody says, "Smile, the world is not that bad" or something? There is a lot of stuff. You know these little incidents can lead to big incidents.

And, unfortunately, such concerns were often validated. Izabela, for example, told me she was "terrified" when she learned that a male student who had been following her around the school was part of a group of young men who had harassed and then sexually assaulted another female student. Fearing for her own safety, she devised ways to protect herself.

> I don't feel comfortable walking where they are, their section of the school ... I have to have at least one person with me or I will take the longer route.

Barbara Houston claims that sexual harassment operates to ensure "that women will not feel at ease"[2] and, certainly, that was the general experience for these students. This feeling of uneasiness in turn had further consequences for their well-being at school.

THE PSYCHOLOGICAL IMPACT

In her groundbreaking work on girls' psychological development, Carol Gilligan has begun to address what she describes as "a startling omission: the absence of girls from the major studies of adolescence."[3] She has made some worrying discoveries. By comparing the voices of eleven- and sixteen-year-old girls, Gilligan has found that the sense of outspokenness and authority that are evident in young girls diminishes as they grow older. The confident eleven-year-old is transformed into an apologetic, hesitant teen-ager who questions her own knowledge and her own sense of authority.[4]

Adolescence seems to be a time when many girls begin to shut down and I believe sexual harassment has a lot to do with this. Sexual harassment can slowly erode young women's confidence and self-esteem and make it difficult for them to develop a positive female identity. Being harassed made Claire feel like "a lesser person" and certainly that was the inherent message in every harassing act she encountered.

It's curious that young women's low self-esteem is recognized as a primary deterrent to their education with little concomitant discussion about why girls get so down on themselves. In a recent radio program entitled "Girls and Math," high school girls were interviewed about their experiences in same-sex and mixed-sex math classes. The students in all-girls classes had developed a positive attitude towards math and were enjoying it more and more all the time. On the other hand, young women in the mixed-sex class complained about the ways male students insulted and berated them and, for this reason, they didn't enjoy being there. (The guys, by the way, were questioned about the young women's accusations and admitted they were true.)

A team of experts invited to respond to the students' comments included a math coordinator from one of the school boards. He was asked what his board was doing to make girls feel different about themselves when it comes to math. His remarks were typical.

> Many schools have offered for students, and especially for girls, study skills, assertiveness training; things that help them build up their own self-esteem.

But girls' self-esteem is not the problem. It is the *result* of the problem. Chalking up girls' problems to their low self-esteem is like diagnosing someone as being sick: it begs the question "Why?" Girls' lower self-esteem is a logical response to the destructive behaviour levelled against them and the best way to make them feel better about themselves is to treat them like worthwhile human beings.

Sexual harassment is "one of the most important ways in which inequality impacts on women's mental health"[5] and the emotional consequences get played out in a variety of ways. The psychological trauma that can result from sexual harassment has a lot to do with women's inability to articulate their experiences in a language that accurately reflects their feelings about these harassing events. For example, much of the behaviour women experience as demeaning, degrading and, at times, terrifying, is distorted when it is filtered through a dominant male discourse that sees these acts as nothing more than harmless and natural male behaviour.

Many women adopt this rendition of their events if it is the only interpretation available to them. But this creates a kind of splitting of their internal and external selves as, overtly, they pretend to dismiss, tolerate — even enjoy — harassing incidents while, at the same time struggling with feelings of humiliation, anger, and terror that arise from these same events.

Female students often responded to harassing incidents in ways that were in sharp contrast to their inner feelings. Ruth said she'd get upset when guys hassled her — but she tried not to show it. Her strategy was never to get angry; instead, she tried to "laugh it off like everybody else." Ironically, this commonly used tactic is often taken as evidence that women really don't mind being sexually harassed.

But the pent-up anger and frustration of many of these young women was released as they recorded incidents in their journals. What triggered Lyla's anger was realizing how often she'd been harassed.

> It made me even more mad when I thought about it. When it happened ... you just kinda go through it. But, then, when I thought about it, I wondered, "Have they been doing this all along?" Then I'd start going over my memories of the things they did to me and I just never noticed.

It's not surprising that the release of this supressed anger came about in a safe and private activity such as writing in a journal rather than as a public display. Jean Baker Miller points out that anger as an acceptable emotion is reserved primarily for people who are members of dominant or powerful groups.[6] This is puzzling when one considers that people in subordinate positions are more likely to be in situations that generate anger as they try to cope with vulnerability, powerlessness, and lack of resources. But when subordinates get angry the power of dominants is threatened because the social inequities that account for their privileged position are in danger of being exposed. This is why anger is encouraged differently in men and women; women's anger is considered aberrant.

> One thing people don't want to hear about is women's anger! Our culture (and others) has a long history of surrounding this topic with dread and denial. With psychological fields, there has been frequent use of such terms as castrating women, and the like, but it is hard to locate any place at which women's anger enters as a "proper" phenomenon. It is virtually always seen as pathological.[7]

Keeping a journal gave these young women licence to think and react without fear of censorship or rebuke. They were safe from the backlash so commonly experienced by women who dare to speak out against sexual harassment.

> Just remembering it, I was getting so mad. I don't get mad when there's people around me and I'm talking about things like now. But if I'm by myself and I'm really thinking about them I think, "They've got some nerve."

The continual suppression of anger can produce feelings of frustration and inaction that increase women's sense of vulnerability and helplessness. And when anger is repressed it gets manifested in alternative ways, such as depression.[8] This may be one reason women are more likely than men to be diagnosed as clinically depressed. And this might also explain why, for students like Fatima, keeping a journal seemed almost therapeutic: it became a safe place to express her anger.

> I [got] my feelings out more, like you get angry ... and then when I wrote them down again I just got more out of it. It helps me to relax.

The splintering of the self that occurs when young women try to suppress their true feelings can have consequences for their developing identities. When young women have such a fragmented sense of themselves, they risk losing control over their self-definition. Tanya, for example, changed her whole image in response to male students' allegations that she was a slut.

> I used to listen to heavy metal, my hair used to be long, I used to have the jacket and the pants, everything …. When I went to another school it was alright the way I dressed because everybody did it …. Now all those clothes are in the garbage. Because they wouldn't leave me alone. They kept calling me a slut.

When students like Jessica dressed for school, a big factor in their choice of clothing was the anticipated response of male peers.

> Sometimes, I think, "I can't wear that to school because it's very showy" … and I think, "Oh, my God, I can't dress like this, either." There's no right way to dress.

Ruth said it really didn't matter what she wore because "the guys will comment on … whatever you have on." But, to be safe, most female students don't wear anything "too outlandish."

Traditionally, researchers have recognized that the taking on of male-defined values and perceptions and the renouncing of the self seemed to be a big part of girls' passage into adolescence and womanhood. What is most astonishing, however, was the general consensus that such a process was normative. This is because many theories of adolescence either don't deal with females at all or are based on the notion that the male develops an identity, while the identity of the female is determined by the male or males in her life.

It is only recently, with the work of researchers like Carol Gilligan, Laura Brown, Lyn Mikel Brown, Trudy Hanmer, Nona Lyons, and Annie Rogers that we've realized how young women have been harmed by the widespread use of these androcentric theories. By listening to girls' voices, these researchers have learned that adolescence is a time when girls' knowledge and learning begins to go underground:

> As the phrase "I don't know" enters our interviews with girls at this developmental juncture, we observe girls struggling over speaking and not speaking, knowing and not knowing, feeling and not feeling, and we see the makings of an inner division as girls come to a place where they cannot say or feel or know what they have experienced — what they have known and felt.[9]

Until recently, this repression of girls was considered part of their normal development.

When do girls shut down? In a society where women are so devalued there is little positive affirmation of a female identity in any stage of a woman's life. A young woman's developing sense of herself as a valuable and autonomous person comes up against a formidable block when her sexual development becomes visible and she realizes the danger in her developing sexuality. Elizabeth Stanko explains it this way.

> ... As soon as women begin pubescent development they actually begin to see male behavior toward them change. Adolescent girls are met with comments, glances, whistles .... Fending off male sexuality, much of what is initially welcomed, the young girl also learns that she cannot always control sexual encounters she engages in. She also learns that if anything happens, she is to blame ...[10]

Sexual harassment reminds girls that they are always at risk and, so, like Ruth, Tanya and Jessica, they begin to take on an identity that offers them more protection. In the end, however, they can lose a sense of who they really are. Carol Gilligan warns that adolescence is "a time when girls are in danger of drowning or disappearing."[11] And with each harassing incident they move one step closer to oblivion.

THE PHYSICAL IMPACT

Being harassed at school created an anxiety that affected some students in physical ways. Zoe was so nervous about a group of male students who were always demeaning female students that her "stomach would turn" when she had to pass by them as she walked through school hallways. Sometimes male students' crude jokes about "broads," "tits" and "condoms" were so repugnant that Beth felt nauseous and was reduced to tears: "I was crying later and I didn't feel like going to any of my classes ..." Such physical reactions are not uncommon. Connie Backhouse and Leah Cohen have found that physical ailments such as nausea, headaches, muscular spasms, insomnia and hypertension can be symptoms of the "sexual harassment syndrome"[12] that many women suffer as a result of the frustration and tension they suffer when they are constantly fending off sexually harassing behaviour.

There is a growing awareness that women's preoccupation with their body weight starts early and gets played out in ways that range from periodic monitoring of food intake to perpetual dieting to full-blown anorexia and bulimia. In a study of adolescents, researchers found that 83 percent of girls who worried that they were too fat were within the normal range of weight for their height.[13] Based on statistics like these, researchers like Janet Surrey are convinced that:

> ... Eating patterns and associated psychological disturbance originate most often during the teenage and young adult years ... It appears that this is a critical period for researching the physical and psychological development of young women in today's cultural context.[14]

Researchers have yet to seriously consider the obvious link between sexual harassment and disordered eating as they explore the cultural factors that account for young women's loathing of their own bodies. This connection is evident in Catherine Steiner-Adair's account of her work with Ariel, a young adolescent who, when she first came to therapy, was depressed, suicidal and bulimic:

> Like other teenage girls with eating disorders, she truly hates herself as well as her body. She knows that she hates being a girl as well: "I hate being a girl, I wish I was a boy. It sucks being a girl. You get totally put down, sexually harassed, ditzed."[15]

One female student explained that when guys at school call her "cow" or "pig" she stops eating for a few days. In my recent work in elementary schools, girls tell me that when boys compare them to pictures of the buxom sunshine girls that drape the pages of newspapers or tease them with comments like "You're so flat the wall are jealous," they start to feel uneasy about their developing bodies. As one student explained: "I feel bad about my body and I wish that I was a boy."

In addition to having a detrimental effect on their physical well-being, the experience of being sexually harassed caused the young women to limit their physical movement around the school. Many would avoid areas of the school where they were likely to be verbally or physically hassled; hallways in particular were identified as sexual harassment zones that were to be bypassed if at all possible.

> A lot of girls won't walk past hallways, 'cause they know guys will be there, grabbing their arms or saying, "Oh, come here baby." Most girls won't walk through a particular hallway because of those gestures, you know.

Some students developed alternate routes around the school that would limit the possibility of being sexually harassed.

> They'll keep on doing it every single day .... They'll say, "What a nice ass." You get to the door and you decide which way you should go .... I don't want to go past them, so I go through the other side of the door. I take the longer way.

When they were unable to avoid a known sexual harassment area in the school, many students tried to ensure they weren't alone.

> I won't walk down the main hall by myself. Not if there's a bunch of guys standing there. I'll go with one or two of my friends but none of us will walk through the halls ourselves .... They all stand in a line and they wait for people to come so they can cut them down.

As Joan put it, "Girls need to stick together, for protection."

THE ACADEMIC IMPACT

The undermining of young women's confidence and the threat to their personal security has serious implications for their education. As Adrienne Rich points out, because our minds and bodies are inseparable, when young women fear for their safety at school, their minds are also in mortal danger.[16] So, being sexually harassed can also have a big impact on girls' performance in school.

The experience of sexual harassment influenced the academic performance of these students in two significant ways. First, in an effort to avoid harassing behaviour, they limited their participation in class discussions and their enrolment or attendance in various courses. Zoe monitored the behaviour of male students in her classes for the first month of school to see how they responded to female students. During this observation period she didn't speak up in class.

> ... Some of those guys will be in my class and I don't know what they will do ... In some of my classes they didn't do anything 'cause the teacher was there and I was sitting on the opposite side. But if they did ... I don't know ... what to say to guys when they embarrass me and mostly in front of everybody.

At least three young women complained about male students disrupting their class presentations. Helen described what happened during her talk on Nellie McClung, a famous woman historian.

> I did a presentation on Nellie McCLung. I dressed up as her. It was a really neat presentation ... And then one guy ... said something that made the kids at the back laugh, so I figured it was a stupid comment and that bugged me. From then on I wasn't as assured as I would have been if I had had their undivided attention.

Clare became embarrassed and "goofed up her lines" when a group of male students chanted "airhead, airhead" as she spoke to the class. She said this type of behaviour happened so often that some female students were "afraid to get up ... and do presentations."

Sometimes, students would skip classes to avoid being subjected to anti-female remarks or taunting behavior. The guys in one of Zoe's classes would often make disparaging comments about women and, so, as she explained, "I didn't really much go to that class ... that's why I didn't do well." In a few cases, the young women had withdrawn from courses rather than put up with the hassling they got in class.

Some students who were subjected to extreme forms of harassment felt they had no option but to transfer schools. In speaking of a close friend, Izabela explained:

> She didn't want to leave, she likes [this school] but there was nothing else she could do. The school wasn't going to do anything and she was not going to be subjected to this kind of harassment for another year ... You never know where it might lead to.

About three years ago I attended a sexual harassment workshop where a teacher reported that at least twenty female students had transferred from her school because they had suffered severe sexual harassment.[17] And Beth, a participant in this study, documented a series of harassing incidents in her journal and, then, recorded the following comment: "I hate school and I hate them getting off easy, while I go through pain and hurt. Maybe an all girls school would be better for me." I heard later that she had left the school.

A second way that sexual harassment affected young women's school performance was through the constant distractions they experienced as they tried to focus on their school work. For example, Alison complained that the persistent rubbing and poking that she got from a male student in class made it difficult to hear what the teacher was saying.

> Actually, it did have an effect, and I've been thinking about this. I would try to listen but he'd say things to me. When he did that I'd be trying to concentrate on what the teacher was saying. But I couldn't because he was bugging me.

In some cases, the vulgar remarks made by male students in courses were so disturbing and persistent that some young women dreaded going to class.

> A guy who sits next to me was talking about his own idea of an advertisement: "I should make an advertisement for *Playboy*. Put a nice body on the cover. A fucking broad with big tits and ass." ... I don't want to be in this class anymore. I want to run out and just leave this class. I'm tired of hearing this crap.

Jennifer found it difficult to concentrate on her work in one class because male students were constantly "making comments about girls they've had sex with." She worried that some of their remarks were in reference to her.

> When you are doing your work and they're talking about you, you feel like they are staring at you. You are constantly looking up and you never get anything done. So that means you just stand there and look at them to make sure they're not looking at you.

Even when she moved to a different seat in the classroom, Dora's friend continued to be hassled by a male student.

I can say right now it affects her studies because she had to get moved. He was sitting in back of her so she got moved to the front of the classroom. And he still teases her from where he is, throws paper at her, writes little notes.

Although the incidents I have highlighted in this section occurred in the classroom setting, it was the overall experience of sexual harassment within the school that created a debilitating learning environment for female students. As Chen put it:

Sometimes a little thing will last the whole day and you can't concentrate. You keep thinking about it over and over again.

In thinking about the ways that sexual harassment affected her academic performance, Alison summarized it this way: "If there was no sexual harassment at school I could get straight A's, I'm sure of it."

When compared to the results of a study on sexual harassment in high schools conducted by the American Association of University Women, the responses of these young women are pretty typical. In the AAUW survey, female students reported that their most common reaction to sexual harassment was fear and that the consequences of being harassed included "not wanting to go to school," "not wanting to talk as much in class," "finding it hard to pay attention in school," "staying home from school or cutting a class," "making a lower grade in class," and "thinking about changing schools." [18] These comments are depressingly similar to those of the students recorded here.

To say that every female student is devastated by sexual harassment would be a gross exaggeration, but few are unscathed by the persistent taunting, teasing and pestering girls get at school. It's not surprising that each of these young women monitored their behaviour in some way because of the experience or threat of being sexually harassed, even when they claimed that a lot of the hassling didn't bother them. Such self-regulation becomes such a component of women's everyday lives that most of us do it unconsciously.

Sandra Butler has a simple exercise that demonstrates this. In mixed-sex groups, she asks men and women to write down five things they do to avoid sexual assault. When I tried this with university students the men were stumped, while most women wrote continually until the time was up. It was astounding to hear the variety of self-protective strategies the women had developed: not going out at night, taking cabs instead of public transit, buying baggy clothes, not drinking on dates, travelling with a male, buying boots with steel toes, taking a self-defense course, and on and on. Until they did this activity, most women admitted they hadn't thought much about all the safety measures they incorporated into their everyday lives; in fact, many would have said they didn't worry about sexual assault. This is because women are expected to take precautions. In the same way, much of the defensive behaviour adapted by these young women was considered normal. Of course, guys will hassle you if you walk down the hallway. No problem, just go the other way.

In answering the question "How does sexual harassment affect girls' learning?" Carrie Herbert summarizes it this way.

> As with adult women, depression, fear and feelings of guilt combine to act on the person making them miserable, lacking confidence and unable to perform at their best. Women's strategies which could more productively be used elsewhere are spent on avoidance strategies or tense interactions.[19]

The avoidance strategies developed by these students as they attempted to manoeuvre their way through a hostile learning environment had negative implications for their education. The practices of avoiding hallways, monitoring clothing, not participating in class, skipping classes, dropping courses, and leaving school offered them some protection from harassment — but also made school an unwelcome, even menacing place. In most cases, however, these students had few alternatives. They were struggling to deal with a problem that had yet to be acknowledged by those entrusted with their education. So, when it came to fending off sexually harassing behaviour, these young women were on their own.

EXPRESSIONS OF RESISTANCE

The self-protective behaviour the female students adopted as safeguards against males' harassing behaviour should be recognized as positive expressions of their strength and resistance. Their reaction to being sexually harassed usually depended upon their assessment of the volatility of the situation. In many cases, the young women's decision not to respond in an overt way was a strategy they used to secure their own safety. It wasn't, as is often assumed, a sign of their tacit acceptance of the harassing act.

Female students didn't respond directly to harassment when they felt the abuse might "have gotten worse" had they done so. Lyla explained why she didn't confront the male students who frequently hassled her when she entered the school.

> I just walk right by because they usually hang around in front of the school yard. I won't say anything...I know a lot of them have been doped up or they've been drinking. I really don't pay much attention. I think it would be more of a hassle if I did say something than just ignore it, because they'd start bugging me. They'll say, "What's your problem, bitch?" or something like that. "We're just teasing, don't you know it? Can't you take a compliment?" They'll put it in such a sarcastic way that it will make you feel really bad, as if you're making a big deal out of it.

Girls and women are often considered to be the passive recipients of abuse. But to label Lyla's response as passive would be inaccurate. As Jean Baker Miller points out, "One never merely passively receives; one also reacts."[20] Much of what gets labelled as passivity is women's self-protective monitoring of threatening situations.

> Reaction can take many forms …. Women have often heard more than what was overtly stated and have gone through a more complex processing of information. Part of this processing … include[s] the knowledge that one had better not react differently and honestly to what has been said and done. This avoidance of direct expression has been interpreted as evidence of inherent passivity.[21]

There is evidence that girls develop the listening, monitoring and observational skills that are commonly mislabelled as "passivity" at a young age and researchers have found that girls are more likely to display these skills when they are involved in mixed-sex, as opposed to same-sex, activities. When she reviewed the play patterns of children, Eleanor Maccoby found that:

> … When paired with boys, girls frequently stood on the sidelines and let the boys monopolize the toys. Clearly, the little girls in this study were not more passive than the little boys in any overall trait-like sense. Passivity in these girls could be understood only in relation to the characteristics of their interactive partners. It was a characteristic of girls in cross-sex dyads.[22]

Maccoby also noted that the ways boys communicated with girls included commands, threats, boasts, heckling and derogatory remarks, behaviour that is clearly harassing. It seemed that the alleged "passivity" of the girls was, in fact, a strategy they used to avoid rough treatment from the boys.

> The behavior of girls implied that they found the presence of boys to be less aversive when an adult was nearby. It was as though they realized that the rough, power-assertive

behavior of boys was likely to be moderated in the presence of adults, and indeed, there is evidence that they were
right.[23]

In same-sex groups, then, boys and girls were equally active.
However, the aggressive and demeaning ways boy communicated with girls in mixed-sex groups sent girls scurrying to the
sidelines for protection, while the boys continued their activities. Such defensive behaviour on the part of girls and women
is often misnamed as "passivity."

The fear of being abused can prompt girls and women to
develop self-protective strategies that limit their mobility and
suppress their verbal expression, as was the case with many of
these students. But this behaviour shouldn't be construed as
their passive acceptance of abuse. On the contrary, such tactics are often carefully crafted responses designed to reduce
the impending threat of violence.

For example, the reason most of these young women didn't
report incidents of sexual harassment was to protect themselves
from further abuse. Dora described the situation of a close
friend who was being hassled at school by a male student.

> She's always got a friend with her. I asked her, "Why won't
> you ever walk around the school alone?" She said,
> "Because I'm scared of a male student." I said, "If you're
> scared of him why don't you say something to your
> teacher?" She answered, "Because I know if I say some-
> thing the male student is going to turn around and come
> back after me." And it's true, that's how the guys are.

Such concerns weren't unfounded. In one school, a young
woman who had been assaulted by a group of male students
reported the incident to the vice-principal and, when the
guys found out she had "snitched," they began a relentless
campaign to publicly demean her.

> They started calling her names right in front of her
> friends, like "bitch," "white whore" and everything and

they even did it deliberately in a crowd in public to make her stand out. It was very difficult for her and for us too. We knew the guys. We were originally all friends.

The backlash suffered by some young women who dared to confront or report harassing behaviour warned others they could be subjected to similar treatment if they tried to do the same. As a result, those students who did speak out often felt isolated because other young women were too intimidated to offer their support. This was the situation in one class when a group of male students began "taking cheap shots" at a female student who was arguing that pornography degraded women.

> At first the guys started making legitimate arguments, but then they got really personal in referring to her. They said, "Maybe you're pissed off because you don't have the looks for it or you don't have the body for it." She was arguing but what I got mad at was that a lot of girls didn't say anything even though they agreed with what she was arguing for .... The bell rang and all of us just left .... The girls walked out and they didn't say anything and she was the last one to leave.

Lyla said that she and many of the other young women agreed with this student's viewpoints on pornography, but they "were afraid to speak up" because they feared they would suffer similar attacks.

Considering the hostile situation, the silence of the other young women can be seen as a reasonable strategy for securing their own safety. But, at the same time, it acted as a wedge that deepened the divisions between them. In such a threatening environment, these young women knew that backing up their assaulted classmate could put them at great risk. So the young woman was left to fend for herself while her female classmates looked on. When a show of mutual support is such a scary thing for young women, the potential for their collective power is squashed. But, at the same time, their self-protective silence only strengthens the collective power of the young men.

When they felt safe to do so, most young women openly objected to being harassed. Previously mentioned strategies such as monitoring clothing, not participating fully in classes, and dropping courses, were practical ways the students avoided being harassed. But challenging harassers directly was much more empowering. Beatrice told me, "When I confronted [this guy] for smacking me on my ass ... I felt good." Beth excused herself from class because everyone had heard her angry rebuttal to a male student's demeaning comments, and she was embarrassed. But she told me, "I felt better after I left just knowing I got the last say." Beatrice was often direct with guys who hassled her: "What the fuck are you doing? ... I don't like that. Don't do it." Males who whistled at Dora were likely to get a strong reaction.

> If guys whistle at me ... to get my attention I won't look. I'll turn around and say, "You either call me by my name or don't call me at all."

Some young women tried to point out how a particular type of behaviour made them feel.

> He said, "I didn't know she was that easy." I turned around and said, "That's rude what you're saying. You shouldn't be talking about her like that." And then I added, "You're making me sick. Please stop it."

Helen explained a new tactic she had devised for dealing with harassers. Although she was still "trying it out" she claimed that it was "really working."

> I don't tell them right there. I just kind of look at them and acknowledge what they say with a nod of my head, but I don't really say anything. And then afterwards when I can get them by themselves — because it's really stupid to tell them to shut up there because that's what they want —

I confront them and ask them why they did it. Did I do anything to inflict it? And so on and so forth. It's better than just yelling at them in public. I've talked to my teachers when it's a problem in the classroom. But I don't start yelling at them because that doesn't really help.

Sometimes students would attempt to disarm their harasser by surprising him with a comeback or embarrassing him in front of friends.

Before I would just keep walking. Now I'll say some sort of comment back, but nothing to provoke them. But I'll say something to shut them up ... I guess they're surprised that I actually say something ... I was in the hall once and this Chinese guy goes, "Oh, I love you." And I said, "Are you that hard up? You don't even know me?" His friends are all, "Whoa!" I saw him the next day and nothing ... nothing at all.

But, unfortunately, not all encounters were so successful. Guys would typically laugh off young women's verbal protests or claim they were being "too sensitive" and "couldn't take a joke." But even when the young women resorted to more physical responses, the harassment often persisted.

I said, "Stop it," but he doesn't. He keeps pulling, he is so tight ... and he just keeps grabbing on to me ... I go, "Stop it." One time I stepped on his foot and he still pulled. What's his problem?

Clearly, these students were not passive victims of harassing behaviour. They were, however, the casualties of an educational system that failed to protect them.

The costs of young women's endless vigilance and constant violation at school are perhaps immeasurable and extend far beyond the educational setting. Helen believed that female students would be more likely to achieve their full potential if they didn't have to face "the intimidation factor."

According to Lyla, young women begin to tread cautiously through the world when they come to see sexual harassment as an inevitable part of their lives.

> Sexual harassment has an effect on how you feel anywhere, especially at school .... If you get it at school, then you're always aware of it when you're out in public. You're always thinking, "I get teased for this at school. It's probably going to be the same thing here."

But something happened to these young women over the course of their involvement in this study. Their voices that had initially "cracked with qualification"[24] became strong and determined as they shared common experiences. Beatrice explained it this way:

> The difference is now ... I want things to change. Before if this happened I would ignore it .... Now it's like, "That's awful ... change, change, change."

They were becoming a force to be reckoned with.

Chapter Six

EDUCATING FOR CHANGE

SEXUAL HARASSMENT is clearly a debilitating experience for female students, but school officials can play a big role in changing this. So far, not much has been done to raise awareness about the problem of sexual harassment in schools. If this doesn't change, students like Izabela wondered, "How is anybody supposed to know about it?" When students, teachers, and school administrators aren't familiar with the term "sexual harassment" or if they don't recognize the range of harassing behaviour, the taunting, teasing and tormenting of girls in schools will continue.

Before outlining strategies for eliminating sexual harassment in schools, I want to relay what the students told me about the ways their school officials have responded to sexually harassing behaviour. Their comments fall into three categories: (1) tolerance, (2) ineffective responses and (3) effective responses.

TOLERANCE FOR HARASSMENT

Only a few educators directly harassed female students, but many participated in a tacit way by tolerating this behaviour in their schools. This made it difficult for the young women to stand up to their harassers. As Beth put it, "How do you deal with something like this when the person who is in charge ... doesn't do a thing about it?"

When teachers overlooked the harassing behaviour that went on in their classrooms, the students often felt defence-less and abandoned. Tanya described how she continually looked to the teacher for support as she tried to fend off the demeaning antics of a male intruder in one of her classes.

> The supply teacher was there and he was standing at the back of the classroom like some zombie staring at the front board. I was sitting there doing my work and I was trying to study. And this guy came into the class. I'd never seen him before. He came over and sat in front of me .... So I am reading my book and he says, "Oh, what are you studying there?" ... He grabs the book ... and I say, "Can I have my book back?" ... And he says, "Oh, no, no, no. I'll just keep this for now." And everybody is just sitting there looking at me ... I still had my notes in front of me and I was trying to look at them ... He looks into my bag and he's got my student card .... He said, "Oh yeah, this is a really bad picture of you." ... I said, "Give me that back!" He is holding me and he is taller than me .... And then he says, "Oh look, she is getting nervous, she is blushing." ... And he put the book down his pants and he said, "If you want it, come and get it." ... I kept looking at the teacher and he wasn't doing anything. He was just sitting there. I thought, "Thanks a lot."

Zoe was angry and bewildered when the guys who were hassling her in class got off scot free while she was admonished for confronting them.

> I was in grade eight, and we were taking family studies ....
> So there were these guys and I was wearing a very short skirt .... They were trying to lift my skirt from the back 'cause it was short and it was hanging down. And I stood up and said, "Stop it!" I got really mad. It happened every

day for about a week. And I got in trouble from the teacher for interrupting the class. When I told her the story, she said, "Well, you shouldn't interrupt my class." ... But I am not going to sit there and let them touch me, when I don't want to be touched. And I got in trouble .... So I went back to my seat and I told them don't do that and they still kept on doing it and I had to sit there and just take it ... In that class I didn't wear skirts anymore, I'll tell you. I tried to wear pants.

When teachers failed to challenge harassing behaviour, some students saw it as a mark of their general lack of concern for issues that pertained to young women. Being told to "forget about" the fourteen women who were killed in Montreal and having to skip class in order to see a school presentation on date rape are other incidents that led the students to conclude that some teachers just "don't care."

Other students felt that the problem was their teachers' inability to contain the harassing behaviour of male students in their classroom.

In class ... the guys, they'll all have this idea that girls should be in the kitchen doing their work. The teacher, if it's a male teacher, doesn't say anything. He just says, "That's enough." ... He sits there and he watches and he doesn't have a smile on his face or anything. He's just sort of given up hope. He doesn't say anything to make them stop.

Of course, teachers are unlikely to have the knowledge and the support to deal with sexual harassment if the problem isn't taken seriously by those in positions of authority within the school. These students felt that many administrators wouldn't deal with harassing behaviour unless they were pressured.

For example, in the following scenario, female students were complaining about male students holding up scoring cards to rate young women as they passed through the hallway. The principal's initial reaction was to reprimand the young women for "yelling" and then to dismiss the incident by promising to deal with it later. It was a student and a teacher who insisted that he deal with the situation immediately.

> Finally the principal comes along, "Could you please cut down on the noise? We're having a student council meeting in there." Several young women were trying to explain what happened. He said, "Calm down, you're yelling too much. There's no need for yelling." Ms _____, a teacher, explained the situation to the principal. He said, "Put those signs away. We'll deal with this later." But then I said, "Why not deal with it now?" Ms _____ said, "Why not deal with it now?" The principal was embarrassed and said, "C'mon boys, come with me into my office." ... It really bothered me when the principal didn't take this situation seriously. He made it sound like the student council meeting was more important than this. If I had not told him to deal with it, he would have gone on with his business and nothing would have been done about it.

But even when they thought school officials would respond, many students said they'd be reluctant to report sexual harassment. What concerned them was their school's record in handling previous complaints.

INEFFECTIVE RESPONSES

There were two main reasons the young women hesitated to report sexual harassment. Their first concern was that the strategies schools used to deal with harassers weren't very effective. Jennifer explained why she decided to drop a course rather than complain about a teacher who was always making disparaging comments about women.

> The only thing you can do about it is go to the office and record it. But I think it has been reported so many times

they're just tired of listening to it ... I think he got a warning .... He's changed a bit but not a lot. People have just said, "Well, they gave him a warning, he hasn't changed much, so I'm not going to bother with him. I'm just going to drop his course."

Izabela who found herself in a similar situation said there were already "several complaints" against one teacher, but the problem persisted. She figured another complaint wouldn't make any difference: "I don't think anyone can change him, the way he is."

The second reason the students didn't report sexual harassment was their concern that doing so would only make the problem worse. One student got "psyched out" when she was repeatedly asked to describe her harassment and abuse to various school officials.

I didn't think the school handled it very well because they had several meetings talking to her and she got passed along from one vice-principal to another. The first vice-principal was a guy and he said, "Well, you should talk to Ms ____ because she would know better about this stuff."

Lyla, a friend of this young woman, described the problems with this procedure.

I don't think what the first vice-principal did was ethical. When a student is in trouble you don't just hear it and then put it aside. I think there's a reason he did that. He's male and this was a male thing. So he was uncomfortable with the situation and he made her feel very uncomfortable, which she already was. So I think that the vice-principal should have more knowledge. If he was truly inexperienced and he didn't want to deal with it he should have been more direct about it. He should have been more understanding ... he should have been more gentle to her, I think. That's what got her very scared ... because she was expecting something good to happen. But what happened was that it just dragged on and made things worse. So she won't say anything anymore. She doesn't trust her peers anymore. She doesn't trust the school system at all.

This young woman's trauma was intensified when she was called to a meeting with the vice-principal only to discover her assailants sitting in the office.

> She didn't even go into the office .... She was really scared and she was very pissed off that the vice-principal did that. That put my friend in a very bad position because the guys did not have charges pressed against them. Therefore they could do what they wanted and she was scared. After that, until the end of school ... her friends walked her home, walked her to school. She was never alone, even in school she was with somebody. We would make sure we would walk her to class, from class to lunch .... She transferred to another school.

The school officials had acted on the young woman's complaint, but the situation had been handled in a way that left her feeling even more distressed and vulnerable. When those in positions of responsibility in schools aren't educated about sexual harassment, and when they have no standard procedures for dealing with harassing incidents, their responses to female victims can be harmful. For this young woman, having to explain the incidents to a number of school officials was tantamount to re-living the abuse over and over again. Because she was unwilling to press legal charges, the school "didn't do anything" about the male students and they in turn harassed her even more as a reprisal for having reported them. The only way she could get away from the harassment was to leave the school.

EFFECTIVE RESPONSES

Incidents of sexual harassment weren't always ignored or handled poorly by teachers and school administrators. Some young women thought their school officials did a good job of handling student complaints.

There were three ways educators responded effectively to student reports of sexual harassment: (1) confronting the harasser directly; (2) implementing school rules that limit harassing behaviour and; (3) initiating and supporting educational programs about sexual harassment.

When school officials directly confronted harassers, the abusive behaviour often ended or, at the very least, significantly diminished. Helen found that a few of her teachers were "really good about this stuff" and always took her complaints seriously. She gave me an example:

> For instance, I told you about the guy in my English class … he always say stupid things and stuff like that. I talked to my English teacher and she said, "Well, this is really a problem and a vital concern of yours and I'll talk to the guy." And so she did. He came up to me the next day and said that he didn't realize that he'd made such a big impact on me. So little things do work.

In another case, the anti-female comments a teacher made in class stopped, after he was required to meet with school administrators and a group of female students. According to Zoe, "He was different in the meeting and he is different now …. He is still in the school, but he doesn't say these comments."

One school had implemented a rule that prohibited the display of visual material that could be considered degrading to men or women. This included the nude or semi-nude pictures of women that male students often hang in their lockers. The consequence for violating this rule was serious: suspension from school. Dora thought this was a good rule, because she had always found such material disturbing, particularly when male students used photos of women in provocative positions to tease her.

Before I just didn't bother looking at it. I just put my head down and walked away ... Now it makes me feel so much better about myself because I know that I won't have people interfering with me ... saying things like, "Oh, yeah, she's so much into it."

A third way schools were confronting this problem was through the implementation of educational programs designed to address the general problem of violence against women. For example, some educators had invited theatre groups to come into the school to do plays about date rape. Because of activities like these, the young women believed that everyone in the school was "becoming much more aware" of these issues.

One school board developed workshops on sexism for both male and female students. The two groups met separately to discuss topics such as sexual harassment and other forms of violence by males and then came together to strategize about ways to deal with the problem. Dora noticed a big change in the guys who had attended these sessions.

I think it's a great idea the guys went. It gave them more understanding about how guys treat girls and they have more respect now for girls .... There's a big change in all of them.

Just by virtue of participating in this study, these schools had opened up a forum for the discussion of sexual harassment. By sanctioning the students' involvement in the various projects that were associated with the research for this book, school officials publicly proclaimed their support for these young women and declared their willingness to address the problem of sexual harassment. Only a small number of young women from each of the schools was involved in our study but, as Helen discovered, the impact of this work extended far beyond the individual participants.

I've noticed people are taking action .... Before I felt that sexual harassment was just a fact of life. Therefore why bother making a stink about it. I guess having something official helped me to realize that this is real. It's not just a petty concern and more attention should be paid to it. [When I went to our meetings] people would ask me, "Where are you going? What are you doing?" And I would tell them .... And they'd say, "Well, is it that much of a problem?" From there would stem different discussions. A lot of guys are learning from our conversation(s).

CREATING POLICY

What we need is a strong, public statement that school boards acknowledge the existence of sexual harassment and the development of a policy that will protect students from being sexually harassed. Given the prevalence of sexual harassment in schools and the many ways it interferes with young women's education, it's a real concern that so many school boards haven't implemented a policy that covers female students.[1]

This is perilous for two reasons. First, it demonstrates a lack of institutional support for those students who are experiencing harassment. This leaves young women with limited options; they can either keep silent or seek protection from educators who may or may not have the necessary knowledge and sensitivity to deal effectively with harassing incidents. Currently, even the most supportive school officials have few guidelines to help them handle students' complaints effectively.

But aside from moral principles, policy is important because school boards could be held legally liable if they don't take the issue of student harassment seriously. During 1992, several school districts in the United States paid out high settlements when they were charged with failing to respond appropriately to the sexually hostile environment within their schools. These charges weren't limited to high schools. In May of 1993, a seven-year-old girl won a historic battle when federal investigators determined that her civil rights had been violated because the school didn't deal effectively with the name-calling and unwelcome touching she was continually subjected to on the bus and on the playground.[2]

In Canada, students can take their complaints to the Human Rights Commission if school boards haven't taken reasonable steps to stop harassing behaviour. What is meant by reasonable steps? In Ontario, according to lawyer Karen Crozier, the school board:

> must expend their resources to the point of financial hard-ship before any judge or human rights tribunal can relieve them of their duties .... What help can the commission provide? .... Where there is no wage loss, nominal damages of $3,000 to $5,000 for enduring two to three days of a harassing atmosphere in a workplace are now common. In addition, where an employee is forced out of his or her job and loses wages (or a teen suffers long-term emotional harm) higher damages can be insisted upon.[3]

Having a strong policy in place can limit the likelihood that school boards will be required to pay out high settlements to students who feel they have no recourse but to take their complaints to the Human Rights Commission.

A good sexual harassment policy should detail the kind of behaviour that constitutes sexual harassment, outline report-ing procedures, define penalties, and incorporate an annual review process to ensure the policy is working. But this is only the first step. A policy collecting dust on the shelf of the principal's office won't do much to combat the problem of sexual harassment. This is why the implementation process is so crucial.

For the past year or so I've conducted workshops on sexu-al harassment with students, teachers and administrators in various school boards. I cover three areas: (1) what sexual harassment is, (2) how it feels to be sexually harassed, and (3) what to do about it. When I get to the "what to do" section I'm always astonished by the number of educators and students who have no idea about whether or not their school board has a sexual harassment policy. And, if a policy is in place, nobody seems to know much about it. To be effective, policies need to be posted and publicized, and members of the school community need to be educated about them.

Involving students in the process of policy development is a way of enhancing the strength and potency of the document by ensuring that it is grounded in the experiences, concerns and suggestions of the group for which it has been developed. The young women I interviewed had a lot to say about making policies user-friendly, so that students would know what to do if they were being harassed. For them, the most important component of the reporting process was the availability of a supportive person in the school; their willingness to report hinged on this factor. Tanya believed that:

> If everybody knew there was at least one person you could talk to with problems like this and something would be done, then I think they will go and talk to the person and say this happened to me.

Some students felt that teachers or administrators would be good contact persons; others thought young women would be more comfortable talking to other female students. Helen proposed various options.

> Maybe a person in the school who is knowledgeable in the area [should be available]. I think that's important. But someone who is also sympathetic to the position ... I can understand why a person wouldn't feel comfortable talking to an authority figure. Maybe, first, they could talk to a student that everyone knew, that everybody felt comfortable around. And then that student could go with them to

the principal or the nurse. We have police officers here a couple of mornings every week and people come to them. That is apparently successful.

Teri suggested that a group of students and teachers who "know what they're talking about and know what is going on" could become the resource people for students in the school who are dealing with issues related to sexual harassment. It was assumed that these people would accompany the student to the administrator's office, if she decided to make a formal complaint.

Jessica thought there'd be some young women who wouldn't feel uncomfortable telling *anyone* they were being harassed. She devised a way they could get advice anonymously.

> I think they would be a little bit hesitant and self-conscious to actually present themselves but I think ... some kind of phone-in would be great ... That way you don't know the person, but at the same time you can get advice from a student or maybe a counsellor.

Whatever the options, the young women were clear that the decision to report or not to report an incident of sexual harassment should remain with the targeted student. Ruth described how she would counsel a young woman who was being harassed.

> I wouldn't say, "Go report it, go do it now." I would say, "Would you like to report it? Would you like to speak to the guy yourself? Would you like to speak to a counsellor or a teacher?" I would let her make that choice. I wouldn't tell her what to do.

One word of caution: I'm a little uneasy about policies that build in "conflict resolution" as an informal strategy for dealing with sexual harassment. This procedure is based on the notion that harassing incidents are the outcome of a dispute between individuals. But this depoliticizes the problem. Sexual harassment is an act of power that is most commonly expressed by males over females. Many forms of violence are not conflict based. They are inflicted on certain people merely because they are members of a specific group. For example, young women who are subjected to sexually demeaning comments as they walk down school hallways are being denigrated simply because they are female. If the remedies included in policies aren't sensitive to the gender and power-related issues of sexual harassment, then we've missed the central point.

However, it would be naive to assume that the mere implementation of a policy will resolve the problem of sexual harassment. Although a policy is a statement of institutional support and offers redress to those who are sexually harassed, the ultimate goal of educators should be to change the attitudes that perpetuate sexually harassing behaviour. As Mary Beth put it, "Education is the key to prevention."

EDUCATION AND RESOURCES

Without exception, the most salient theme in the student's comments on ways to eliminate sexual harassment was their conviction that education was the essence of change.

> Educating is the main factor we need now. People ... don't know about harassment and they don't know they can change it or they don't know the actual technicalities of the problems. I think that once they become educated and they realize all the stuff women had to put up with since the beginning of civilization, I think that things would slowly change.

The risk of legal liability has prompted many school boards to strengthen their sexual harassment policies by providing education for all members of the school community. In the Chaska, Minnesota school district, for example,

[A]ll district employees have attended seminars on sexual harassment and students in grade four through twelve [have] studied the issue. Students are helping rewrite pupil handbooks to include a definition of sexual harassment, and high school students serve as members of a new Human Worth and Dignity task force.[4]

For Jessica, education was a way of bringing sexual harassment "out of the closet."

If nobody knows about it, it will just continue. It's like with AIDS or wife abuse. It's gotta come out of the closet sooner or later. If it doesn't, the problems just escalate.

She challenged the commonly expressed allegation that discussions about sexual harassment would be merely "male-bashing."

Some might not be acceptable to such a course, I guess because, in a way, it makes men look bad. But it's not really. It's just trying to make everyone aware of what's going on. It's not trying to say, "Oh, you're bad because you're a man." Both men and women have to be educated about it, just to clear it up.

Students like Beatrice thought there'd be a lot less sexual harassment if teachers knew more about it, because they'd be better able to "correct what happens in the classroom." It should be ensured that education on issues like sexual harassment gets built into the pre-service training, so teachers come into the profession prepared to deal with this kind of behaviour.

The general consensus from these young women was that group discussions were the best format for educating students about sexual harassment. They stressed the need to educate both males and females, but not in the same way. For female students, the group setting should be a forum where they could share their experiences of sexual harassment with other young women. Zoe saw this as a way of breaking down the isolation young women feel, because so many assume "there's no one ... that has the same experience" as they do. In the male groups, the primary focus should be on the impact of their harassing actions on young women. Zoe thought male students needed to know that young women "have feelings and things that they do bother us."

Aside from the difference in focus, another reason the young women believed that male and female students should meet separately was their concern that a mixed-group setting would prevent students from "opening up." From my own experience this is a crucial and relevant point. I've been a participant or a facilitator in a number of mixed-sex sessions where I've witnessed females being silenced by the hostile and intimidating comments of a few males who dominate the group discussions. They usually claim that females are too sensitive, that it's unfair to say that most harassers are male, and that lots of women enjoy this attention or provoke it in some way.

I was recently asked to do a workshop with a mixed-sex group of grade eleven students as part of a school program designed to celebrate International Women's Day. When I asked the teacher whether or not the students had any background on this issue she told me, "No they haven't. And I'm afraid you'll find some of the boys will be very hostile to the information." Mixed-sex educational sessions can be counterproductive. Female students will get a first hand account of the backlash they'll face if they dare to speak out about sexual harassment and male students will get yet another lesson in power and dominance.

I don't think we should dismiss or censor what males are saying. On the contrary, we need to hear their comments so we can deal with any myths, attitudes and stereotypes that inform them. But not at the expense of the girls. Educating males is crucial, but we need to ensure that females aren't being inadvertently silenced in the process.

I disagree with the following recommendation made by Robert Shoop and Jack Hayhow in their recent book on sexual harassment in schools.

> Don't separate males from females during training sessions .... By separating them you perpetuate the misconception that most men are guilty of harassment, that only women are victims, and that this is a divisive issue, a battle of the sexes.[5]

But men *are* more likely to be guilty of sexual harassment, and women *are* more likely to be victims. These facts must be part of any educational program if we want to get at the gender dynamics that are the root cause of this problem. And this is a divisive issue. The purpose of doing education on this topic is to bring males and females closer together by eliminating the destructive behaviour that keeps them apart.

When people tell me that separating the sexes to discuss this issue is promoting segregation, I remind them that young women are avoiding hallways, skipping classes, dropping courses and, generally, not participating fully in school life because they are worried about being sexually harassed. In other words, there *is* sex-segregation in schools. And girl are suffering from it. Providing single-sex groups so that females and males can be supported as they deal with the general and sex-specific issues related to sexual harassment is a way of setting the stage for more positive and productive interactions when they eventually come together. This, as Joan pointed out, should be the ultimate goal.

> I think I would have a group of girls and talk about what bothers them and that I would have a group of boys and talk about what bothers them. Then I'd get the two groups together to talk about it so that they would both know where they stand. I think it's really important because I don't think the boys know what bothers the girls and I think they should.

Students like Zoe were clear that this kind of education shouldn't be limited to high schools: "I think we should have something not only in our school, but in *all* schools...even from kindergarten to grade six."

Other general educational strategies mentioned by the young women included implementing mandatory workshops for all students and teachers, inviting guest speakers to talk about sexual harassment and creating an article or column on sexual harassment for the school newspaper. Ruth thought that posters hung around the school would be a good way to "make everybody know" about sexual harassment. In her words, "If you make a big red poster, everyone will stop and read it." She also wanted the principal to make a general announcement telling students what to do if they are being sexually harassed.

The discussion of sexual harassment shouldn't be limited to scheduled meetings or assemblies. As Helen explained, it should be integrated "into all programs ... stressed in all course outlines" so that it becomes part of the regular school curriculum. Much of this work can be done in an informal way by simply challenging behaviour that has typically been overlooked.

By providing education for teachers and students on sexual harassment, schools can take the lead in eradicating one more barrier that gets in the way of equality for young women both within and beyond schools. But the creation of a harassment-free educational environment isn't likely to be a rapid process. Schools are a microsm of the larger society in which men routinely use diminishment and abuse as a way of expressing their dominance over women. By challenging the attitudes that support sexual harassment we are, in fact, attempting to eliminate one of the tools of a male-dominated culture that is based on the subordination of others. In essence, what we are advocating is radical social change.

At the same time as educators work to end sexual harassment in schools, they will be working against all the social forces that condone it. When we hear that a city official claims that a group of young men who ganged up on a young girl, tore off her swimming suit and sexually assaulted her were merely engaging in horseplay that went too far, or, that parents are protesting their six-year-old son's loss of recess privilege as a principal's too harsh punishment for the boy's part in a playground activity that involved chasing, trapping, and kissing grade one girls, we are reminded that much of this work in schools is going against the social grain. But it's an important start!

In the interim, as we attempt to move female students along the long and rocky road toward equality, we need to offer them some refuge from the forces that operate against them. Male students' appropriation of so much of the physical and intellectual space within the school wears young women down as they attempt to negotiate their way through a threatening educational environment. Young women need a place within the school where they can relax their endless vigilance; they need a place to call their own.

A SEPARATE PLACE

One of the most significant outcomes of this research was the solidarity that developed among the young women as they met to share their experiences of harassment. As Janice Raymond writes in her important book *A Passion for Friends*, the development of strong bonds between women provides them with "a common reference point" so they "do not lose their bearing in the larger world."[6] This kind of grounding occurred in our group meetings as the connections and alliances between the young women began to flourish with their shared stories.

> You've got to put yourself in somebody else's position I
> can understand that person a lot better now because
> they've gone through the same thing that I have .... I can
> associate with them now, maybe not on every level, but on
> one — *as a woman.*

Marilyn Frye is a strong advocate of separate spaces as the key
to women's empowerment. She argues that women get worn
down by the myriad forces that operate against them and so
they need a place:

> somewhat sheltered from the prevailing winds of patriar-
> chal culture [so they can] try to stand up straight for once.
> One needs a place to *practice* an erect posture, one cannot
> just will it to happen. To retrain one's body one needs
> physical freedom from what are in the last analysis physical
> forces misshaping it to the contours of the subordinate.[7]

Separate spaces for young women in educational settings
can take a variety of forms. The most obvious, of course, is
the all-girls school. Recently, feminist researchers have questioned the value of co-ed education for girls and have suggested that female students are more apt to find a friendly and
supportive environment in single-sex schools.[8] Currently
most all-girls schools in North America are privately run and
the high tuition fees prohibit many girls from attending
them. However, with the growing recognition of the many
disadvantages girls face in mixed-sex schools in terms of gender bias in the classroom, lack of female role models, stereo-
typing in curriculum materials, as well as sexual harassment,
concerned parents and teachers are beginning to push for
publicly funded all-girls schools.

In Edmonton, John Masson and other concerned parents
are currently lobbying to win approval for a school for adolescent girls. The reason? Masson worries that his ten-year-old
daughter will "suffer later in school simply because she is
female."[9] According to the Alberta model, the school would

operate through an agreement or "charter" with the local school board or provincial government and would run very much like regular schools. A big difference would be the major role parents and teachers play in key decisions such as educational philosophy and hiring. The school could be in operation as early as 1995.

The demands for all-girls education seem to be growing. In Ontario, some parents braved a night of sub-zero temperatures to be guaranteed the chance to enrol their daughter the following day in the only all-girls school in the Dufferin Peel Separate School Board. A covenant on the lease agreement between the board and the Felician Sisters, who were the founders of the school, guarantees that it remains an all-female setting.

The arguments against all-girls schools range from those who reject the evidence of gender bias in education and consider separate schooling to be preferential treatment for girls, to those who worry that moving girls out of co-educational settings will reduce the pressure for school boards to deal with gender-related problems. Regardless of the setting in which students are schooled, an important long-term goal of any school system should be to achieve gender equity in education.

There are many other ways to provide separate spaces for female students in regular schools. One teacher, for example, ran an all-girls electronics course because he was "fed up with seeing their work sabotaged by the boys."[10] Other schools have developed support groups for those young women who have enrolled in non-traditional courses. In a three-year period following the implementation of such a group, one school found that the drop-out rate of female students had substantially decreased and the number of female students entering non-traditional fields had tripled.[11] So in addition to providing refuge from a hostile learning environment, such groups are also an effective way to increase the number of young women who enter non-traditional fields.

Designating a specific room for female students is another way to encourage strong bonds between young women. The scheduling of all-female events or the organizing of a Young Women's Club are the kinds of activities that could occur in the common room as a way of ensuring that young women take advantage of this separate space. In one school, teachers found that designating a room for female students was a real success; it created:

> a physical space in which [they could] be active, vocal, strong or vulnerable without fear of criticism or anxiety about self-image ... they have become stronger and more confident.[12]

Anyone interested in starting a Young Women's Club will find the work of Toronto teacher Beverly Naveau to be an excellent model. In her article "We Have a Lot to Say: Young Women for Gender Equity," she guides the reader through the development of a girls' club in her elementary school and provides valuable information on ways to structure such a group.

> The goal of the Young Women's Club is to discuss issues of gender equity and to study the impact of gender on the socialization of adolescent girls. Although we concentrate on the school system, we also deal with events in the family and in the broader culture. We attempt to identify connections between problems like violence against women and the marginalization of female students in elementary schools. We try to increase awareness in staff and students of the concept and of the concerns of gender equity, and to give women's issues a higher profile in our school.[13]

The club members have been involved in a long and growing list of activities that include poster campaigns, media studies, poetry and story writing on women's issues, invited guest speakers and self-defence classes for girls. What's most encouraging is the degree of support the club gets from a wide array of individuals and groups connected to their education.

> We have administrative support and initial funding from the Affirmative Action Office of the Board. Parents have expressed their approval of the venture and in some cases sent in newspaper and magazine clippings and messages of encouragement. One of the fathers told his daughter that he thought it was a really good idea for her to belong to such a group, an important affirmation for her. One man, who is the art teacher, designed a logo; the school librarian is ordering materials on gender equity (at the request of the girls) and is helping to mount a campaign entitled "Images of Women" for International Women's Day. We have been promised a meeting room in the school where we can create our own space, store and display materials, and conduct private interviews.[14]

At the same time as we work to alter the hostile climate that surrounds girls in schools, we need to provide an antidote to the debilitating messages that surround them. Bringing young women together is one way to do this. Having the opportunity to share similar experiences can be empowering as young women realize they are dealing with common problems that have little to do with their personal inadequacies. Joan's voice became part of a chorus: "This isn't about me!"

Young women need a place where they can dare to assert themselves so they can feel the power of their collective voices. If they work together, they may have the strength to resist what Carol Gilligan has called the chilling winds of tradition; winds that bring "a message of exclusion — stay out" and "a message of subordination — stay under."[15] Together, young women can claim their rightful place in education.

CONCLUSION

THE TESTIMONIES of these young women paint a grim picture of high school life for female students. Their accounts are clear indicators that something is very wrong with our education system, especially when commitment to gender equity is lauded as a primary objective of most school boards. It seems the road to equality we've carved for female students is fraught with cracks and barriers so that young women move with trepidation, if they dare to move at all. At the same time as they are being diminished by acts of sexual harassment, young women are being told by educators that their opportunities are unlimited. Ironically, many are feeling more confined. Equal opportunity may be increasing young women's access to education, but sexual harassment is keeping them unequal. Their words are bleak reminders of the work we have yet to do if equal opportunity is to become more than a rhetorical term.

Many readers will have a hard time believing that schools can be such toxic places for girls. After reading this work, one educator told me, "I have to confess that I have trouble accepting that every young woman is subject to such harassment." That's not what I'm saying. Not every student I interviewed experienced the extreme forms of harassment that caused Jennifer to drop a course, Beth to change schools and Dora to seek police protection. But they had all been subjected to the ordinary put-downs and objectifying comments that are part of most women's lives. And this had an impact on their education.

It's not my intention to generalize from the experiences of young women in my study to the experiences of all female students. However, sexual harassment does go on in schools and educators need to take a hard look at what's going on in their particular setting. The degree and severity of sexual harassment may vary from school to school. But I think we'd be hard pressed to find any co-educational setting where female students aren't being harassed at all.

Educators can be active in putting an end to sexual harassment and these young women hoped that hearing their stories would convince them to do so. Fatima summed it up this way:

> Sexual harassment does happen in schools .... Girls don't like it and they feel horrible about it. They can do something as teachers to stop it.

There's evidence that school officials are beginning to take on this responsibility. I've spent much of this year working with educators who are eager to find out more about sexual harassment so they can deal with it in their schools. Teachers who have used activities from the educational kit I developed for high schools (see Appendix A) tell me they have noticed a difference in the way their students interact. For example, when grade ten students in a mixed-sex class completed the "Survey on Sexual Harassment" and compared responses, the boys were shocked to realize the extent to which the girls were being harassed at school. As the discussion continued, one of the young men admitted he hadn't realized the harm in some of the comments he made to female students. "From now on," he promised, "I'll be more careful."

In a workshop on sexual harassment, Peg Talacko, Employment Equity Project Leader for the City of York Board of Education, asked female and male students to describe their vision of a harassment-free school. They came up with the following responses:

- Students would be able to concentrate on their work.
- Students would be comfortable with teachers.
- Students would become as one (i.e., less conflict and fighting, more respect).
- There would be better student-teacher relationships.
- No one would make rude comments or jokes to anyone or put anyone down.
- Students could walk down the hall without hearing rude comments.
- People would be able to wear what they want.
- People could talk to one another in a joking way.
- You could feel that you are someone special.
- Teachers would respect each other.
- The school will have a better name and reputation (i.e., attract more students and teachers).
- The school would be like a big family.

This is the kind of learning environment we want for every student. And when we start eliminating sexual harassment in schools, we'll move a little closer to this ideal.

Sexual harassment acts like a wall that blocks young women's movement toward equality in education. In the words of Nan Stein:

> It is time to recognize that sexual harassment, a pervasive, pernicious problem is an obstacle to receiving equal education opportunities and that, in order to receive justice for all, we must take action to prevent and eliminate it.[1]

If we really want to provide an equal education for girls in school, we need to recognize all the forces that work against them. As Lyla so simply put it, "When we start dealing with sexual harassment, that's when equality will begin. That's when we will really start being equal."

EDUCATING ABOUT
SEXUAL HARASSMENT

SINCE COMPLETING this study, I've used the suggestions of the young women to develop educational workshops and resources for high schools. Over the past year, I've also started working on an educational program for students in elementary schools. The program begins with single-sex sessions and works towards bringing male and female students together in a safe and supportive environment.

In the all-female and all-male groups, students learn what kinds of behaviour constitute sexual harassment and they have an opportunity to talk about how this behavior makes them feel. One of the ways I arrive at the gendered nature of sexual harassment with students in same-sex groups is by having them make a list of put-downs that are used against males and females. Inevitably, the list for females is longer. At the end of this session, we rip up the lists as a symbolic gesture of our commitment to eliminating such hurtful words. I remember a particularly poignant moment that followed one of these "ripping" rituals. After tossing the shredded paper in the garbage, one grade five boy turned to the rest of his group and said, "You know, we really need to think about how we talk to the girls." The following week the male and female groups came together to strategize about ways to eliminate sexual harassment in their school.

Some of the exercises I use in the elementary school program are taken from the "Educational Kit on Sexual Harassment" I've developed for high schools. The kit, which is sponsored by the Women's Caucus Against Sexual Harassment at the Ontario Institute for Studies in Education (OISE), is organized into two sections: activities and information. The activity section consists of individual and/or group exercises that are designed to help students and educators (1) identify sexually harassing behavior; (2) understand the negative impact of sexual harassment; and (3) develop strategies for eliminating sexual harassment. The information section of the recently up-dated kit includes sample work-shops and additional resources that may be helpful in organizing a school campaign against sexual harassment, helping individuals respond to incidents of sexual harassment at their school and conducting personal research.

These and other educational materials are available from:

The OISE Women's Caucus Against Sexual Harassment
The Ontario Institute for Studies in Education
11th Floor
252 Bloor St. W.
Toronto Ontario
M5S 1V6

THE AICE MODEL OF EQUAL OPPORTUNITY

As PART OF THE Ontario Ministry of Education funded project on sexual harassment which I conducted with Pat Staton in 1992, Ontario School Boards were surveyed about the formal and informal strategies they had implemented or were developing in the area of gender equity. By far, the most frequently mentioned initiatives were conferences, workshops and presentations on non-traditional careers for girls. But focusing our energy on getting female students into maths and sciences is like chopping down the first few trees of the forest, tossing girls in and expecting them to make it to the other side. With so many obstacles still in their way, many may choose to retreat or not to enter at all. I'm not trying to minimize the importance of encouraging female students to enter non-traditional fields, but this strategy alone won't remove all the barriers they face in their education.

After reviewing the equity initiatives used by various school boards and noting in particular the limited attention given to issues related to the hostile school climate and girls' empowerment, Pat Staton and I developed a more balanced model of equal opportunity which is designed to address the following four issues:

ACCESS – Encouraging equal opportunity in instruction, particularly in fields related to non-traditional jobs. Enabling young women to choose from a range of careers.

INCLUSION– Looking at gender bias in teaching and learning materials both in terms of inclusive language and content.

CLIMATE – Creating an educational atmosphere that is safe and supports equity. Dealing with sexual harassment and violence against women. Looking at what goes on the walls [and] what goes on in the halls.

EMPOWERMENT – Creating a space within the school where young women can develop a sense of solidarity. Providing an antidote to counter the negative messages young women receive both within and beyond their schools.

We call this the AICE model of equal opportunity.

To be effective, programs of equal opportunity must give equal weight to all four components. It's a lot like baking a cake; you can't leave out the eggs or the flour. Similarly, if an equal opportunity program doesn't include all the essential ingredients, it won't be very effective.

By meeting the criteria of the AICE model of equal opportunity, educators will be tackling the specific problem of sexual harassment in schools in its wider context of gender inequity in education. This will move us a giant step closer to making schools more supportive places for female students.

NOTES

INTRODUCTION

1. Walker, W. "Boyd: Sex Harassment Starts in our Schools." *The Toronto Star* (3 May 1994): A1

2. Haynes, P. Letter to Paula J. Caplan, 1991.

3. American Association of University Women. *Shortchanging Girls: Shortchanging America*. Greenberg Lake: The Analyses Group Incorporated, 1990.

CHAPTER ONE

1. Bulzarik, M. "Sexual Harassment in the Workplace: Historical Notes," *Radical America* 12, (July-Aug, 1978): 25-43.

2. Ramazanoglu, C. "Sex and Violence in Academic Life or You Can Keep a Good Woman Down." In *Women, Violence and Social Control*. Eds. J. Hanmer and M. Maynard. London: MacMillan, 1987, 61-74.

3. Stein, N. "Secrets in Public: Sexual Harassment in Public (and Private) Schools." *Work Paper #256*. Wellesley, MA : Center for Research on Women, 1993.

4. Houston, B. "What's Wrong with Sexual Harassment?" *Atlantis* 13, 2 (1988), 45.

5. Pleck, J. *Working Wives/Working Husbands*. Beverly Hills, CA: Sage, 1985.

6. See, for example, Brickman, J., and J. Briere. "Incidents of Rape and Sexual Assault in Urban Canadian Population," *International Journal of Women's Studies* 7, 3 (1984): 195-206; Briere, J., and N. Malamouth, N. "Self-reported Likelihood of Sexually Aggressive Behavior: An Attitudinal vs. Sexual Explanation," *Journal of Research and Personality* 17 (1983): 315-323.

7. Stein, N. ed. *Who's Hurt and Who's Liable: Sexual Harassment in Massachusett's Schools.* Quincy: Massachusetts Department of Education, 1986.

8. Eyre, L. "Misogyny in the Classroom." Paper presented at the Canadian Women's Studies Association of the Learned Societies. Kingston, 1991, 40.

9. See, for example, Bailey, K. *The Girls are the Ones with the Pointy Nails: An Exploration of Children's Conceptions of Gender.* London: The Althouse Press, 1993; Coulter, R. "Gender Socialization: New Ways, New World." Paper prepared for the Working Group of Status of Women Officials on Gender Equity in Education and Training, 1993; Sadker, M., and D. Sadker. *Failing at Fairness: How America's Schools Cheat Girls.* New York: Charles Scribner's Sons, 1994.

10. Stein, N., N. Marshall, and L. Tropp (1993). "Secrets in Public: Sexual Harassment in our Schools." Wellesley, MA : Center for Research on Women at Wellesley College and the NOW Legal Defense and Education Fund, 1993.

11. Staton, P., and J. Larkin. *Sexual Harassment: The Intimidation Factor.* A Report to the Ontario Ministry of Education, 1992, 10.

12. Shakeshaft, C. "A Gender at Risk." *Phi Delta Kappan* (March, 1986), 503.

13. Halson, J. The Sexual Harassment of Young Women. In *Girls and Sexuality: Teaching and Learning* Ed. L. Holly. Philadelphia: Open University Press, 1988, 130-142.

14. Mahony, P. "Sexual Violence in a Mixed Secondary School." In *Learning our Lines.* Eds. C. Jones and P. Mahony. London: The Women's Press, 1989, 157.

15. Miller, J. *Towards a New Psychology of Women,* 2nd edition. Boston: Beacon Press, 1986.

16. Stein, *Secrets in Public: Sexual Harassment in Public (and Private) Schools,* 23.

17. Ibid, p. 24.

18. See, for example, Backhouse, C., and L. Cohen. *The Secret Oppression.* Toronto: MacMillan, 1978; Mercer, S. "Not a Pretty Picture: An Exploratory Study of Violence Against Women in Dating Relationships." *Resources for Feminist Research* (June, 1988): 15-22; Merit Systems Protection Board. *Sexual Harassment in the Workplace: Is it a Problem?* Office of Merit Systems Review and

Studies, Washington, D.C.: United States Government Printing Office, 1981; Ramazanoglu, *Sex and Violence in Academic Life or You Can Keep a Good Woman Down*; Randall, M. *Sexual Harassment.* Toronto: Ontario Women's Directorate, 1987; Safran, C. What Men do to Women on the Job. A Shocking Look at Sexual Harassment. *Redbook Magazine* (November, 1986): 149, 217.

19. Dagg, A., and P. Thompson. *MisEducation: Women & Canadian Universities.* Toronto: OISE Press, 1988, 96.

20. *Observer Review.* "Masters Must Learn that Boys will be Brutes." (6 March 1994): 24.

21. Whitbread, A. "Female Teachers are Women First: Sexual Harassment at Work." In *Learning to Lose: Sexism and Education* Eds. D. Spender and E. Sarah. London: The Women's Press, 1980, 91.

22. Ross, V., and J. Marlowe. *The Forbidden Apple: Sex in the Schools.* Palm Springs: ETC Publications, 1985, 83.

23. Shoop, R. & Hayhow, J. *Sexual Harassment in Our Schools: What Parents and Teachers Need to Know to Spot it and Stop it.* Mass.: Allyn & Bacon, 1994, 24.

24. Ibid; Stein, *Secrets in Public: Sexual Harassment in Public (and Private) Schools.*

25. Boyd, C. "How One Teen Fought Sex Harassment in School." *St. Paul Pioneer Press.* (29 December 1991), 12.

26. Mahony, *Sexual Violence in a Mixed Secondary School,* 187.

CHAPTER TWO

1. Stein, N., ed. *Who's Hurt and Who's Liable: Sexual Harassment in Massachusett's Schools,* 5.

2. Mahony, *Sexual Violence in a Mixed Secondary School,* 175.

3. Spender, D. "Gender and Marketable Skills: Who Underachieves in Maths and Sciences." In *Learning to Lose: Sexism in Education.* Eds. D. Spender and E. Sarah. London: The Women's Press, 1988, 130.

4. Miller, *Towards a New Psychology of Women,* 10.

5. Mahony, *Sexual Violence in a Mixed Secondary School,* 187.

6. See, for example, Shields, S. "Functionalism, Darwinism, and the Psychology of Women: A Study in Social Myth." Reprinted in *Seldom Seen, Rarely Heard: Women's Place in Psychology.*

Ed. J. Bohan. Boulder: Westview Press, 1992, 79-106; Tavris, C. *The Mismeasure of Woman*. New York: Simon & Schuster, 1992.

7. Patrick, 1895, cited in Shields, *Functionalism, Darwinism, and the Psychology of Women: A Study in Social Myth*, 83.

8. Woolley, H. "The Psychology of Sex." *Psychological Bulletin* 11 (1914), 365.

9. Kimball, M. "Saying the Truth: Feminist Empiricism and the Work of Helen Thompson Woolley and Leta Stetter Hollingworth." Paper presented at the Canadian Psychology Meeting, Halifax, 1989.

10. Catell, cited in Lips, H. *Sex and Gender: An Introduction*. California: Mayfield Publishing Co., 1993, p. 149.

11. Shields, *Functionalism, Darwinism, and the Psychology of Women: A Study in Social Myth*.

12. Kimball, *Saying the Truth: Feminist Empiricism and the Work of Helen Thompson Wooley and Leta Stetter Hollingworth*, 8.

13. Ibid.

14. Caplan, P., and J. Caplan. *Thinking Critically About Research on Sex and Gender*. New York: HarperCollins, 1993.

15. Sadker and Sadker, *Failing at Fairness: How America's Schools Cheat Girls*, 1.

16. Ibid.

17. See Gaskell, J., A. McLaren, and M. Novogrodsky. *Claiming an Education: Feminism and Canadian Schools*. Toronto: Our Schools/Our Selves Education Foundation, 1989, p. 36, for a discussion of the Report of the Royal Commission on the Status of Women in Canada (1970).

18. American Association of University Women, *Shortchanging Girls: Shortchanging America*.

19. Sadker and Sadker, *Failing at Fairness: How America's Schools Cheat Girls*.

20. Popaleni, K. "Violence Against Young Women in Heterosexual Courtship: Teaching Girls to Resist." *Canadian Woman Studies/les cahiers de la femme* 12, 1 (1991), 85.

21. Gaskell, McLaren, and Novogrodsky, *Claiming an Education: Feminism and Canadian Schools*, 65.

22. Belenky, M., B. Clinchy, N. Goldberger, and J. Tarule. *Women's Ways of Knowing: The Development of Self, Voice and Mind*. New York: Basic Books, 1986.

23. Rich, A. "Taking Women Students Seriously. In *Lies, Secrets, and Silence*, 237-245. New York: Norton, 1979.

24. Stein, Marshall, and Tropp, *Secrets in Public: Sexual Harassment in Our Schools.*

CHAPTER THREE

1. Kelly, L. "The Continuum of Sexual Violence." In *Women, Violence and Social Control.* Ed. J. Hanmer and M. Maynard. Beverly Hills: Sage, 1987, 114-132.

2. Kelly, L. *Surviving Sexual Violence.* Minnesota: University of Minnesota Press, 1988, 139.

3. Spender, D. *Man-made Language.* London: Routledge & Kegan Paul, 1980.

4. MacKinnon, C. *Sexual Harassment of Working Women: A Case of Sex Discrimination.* New Haven, CT: Yale University Press, 1979, 27.

5. American Association of University Women, *Hostile Hallways: The AAUW Survey of Sexual Harassment in America's Schools.* Washington, DC: Louis Harris and Associates, Ltd, 1993.

6. Eakins, B., and R.G. Eakins. *Sex Differences in Human Communication.* Boston: Houghton Mifflin, 1978.

7. American Association of University Women. *Hostile Hallways: The AAUW Survey on Sexual Harassment in America's Schools.*

8. Pharr, S. *Homophobia: A Weapon of Sexism.* Arkansas: Chardon Press, 1988, 49.

9. Ibid, p. 26.

CHAPTER FOUR

1. Brown, L.M., and C. Gilligan. *Meeting at the Crossroads: Women's Psychology and Girls' Development.* Cambridge: Harvard University Press, 1992.

2. Iversen, H. Personal communication, 1990.

3. Fraser, M.B. "Growing Up in a Sexual Jungle," *Canadian Woman Studies/les cahiers de la femme* 11, 4 (1991), 21.

4. Ibid.

5. Gutek, B. *Sex and the Workplace.* San Francisco: Jossey-Bass Publishers, 1985.

6. Mahony, *Sexual Violence in Mixed Secondary Schools,* 158.

7. The concept of a web of violence is discussed in Popaleni, K. "The Denial of the Self: An Exploratory Study of Young Women's Experiences of Violation within Heterosexual Courtship." Masters of Arts Thesis, University of Toronto, 1990.

8. Levy, B. *Dating Violence: Young Women in Danger.* Seattle: The Seal Press, 1991.

9. Mann, J. *The Washington Post.* (6 May 1988).

10. Miller, B., and Marshall, J. "Coercive Sex on the University Campus," *Journal of College Student Personnel* 28, 1 (1987): 38-47.

11. Bateman, P. "The Context of Date Rape." In *Dating Violence: Young Women in Danger.* Ed. B. Levy. Seattle: The Seal Press, 1991, 94-99.

12. Wise, S., and L. Stanley. Georgie Porgie: *Sexual Harassment in Everyday Life.* London: Pandora Press, 1987, 50.

13. American Association of University Women, *Shortchanging Girls, Shortchanging America.*

CHAPTER FIVE

1. Wise and Stanley, *Georgie Porgie: Sexual Harassment in Everyday Life,* 114.

2. Houston, *What's Wrong with Sexual Harassment?,* 45.

3. Gilligan, C. "Prologue." In *Making Connections: The Relational Worlds of Adolescent Girls at Emma Willard School.* Eds. C. Gilligan, N. Lyons, and T.Hanmer. Cambridge: Harvard University Press, 1990, 1.

4. Prose, F. "Confident at 11, Confused at 16." *New York Times* (7 January 1990): 24, 40.

5. Carmen, Russo & Miller, cited in Koss, M. "Changed Lives: The Psychological Impact of Sexual Harassment." In *Ivory Power: Sexual Harassment on Campus.* Ed. M. Paludi. Albany: SUNY Press, 1990, 85.

6. Miller, *The Construction of Anger in Women and Men.*

7. Ibid, p. 182.

8. Ibid.

9. Brown and Gilligan, *Meeting at the Crossroads: Women's Psychology and Girls' Development,* 4.

10. Stanko, E. Intimate Intrusions. London: Routledge & Kegan Paul, 1986, 2.

11. Gilligan, C. "Teaching Shakespeare's Sister: Notes from the Underground of Female Adolescence." In Making Connections: The Relational Worlds of Adolescent Girls at Emma Willard School Eds. C. Gilligan, N. Lyons, and T. Hanmer. Cambridge: Harvard University Press, 1990, 10.

12. Backhouse and Cohen, *The Secret Oppression*, 45.

13. Feldman, W., P. McGrath, and M. O'Shaughnessy. "Adolescents' Pursuit of Thinness." Abstracted, *American Journal of Dis Child* 140 (1986), 294.

14. Surrey, J. "Eating Patterns as a Reflection of Woman's Development." In *Woman's Growth in Connections: Writings from the Stone Center*. Eds. J. Jordan, A. Kaplan, J. Baker Miller, I. Stiver, and J. Surrey. New York: The Guilford Press, 1991, 239.

15. Adair, C.S. "When the Body Speaks: Girls, Eating Disorders & Psychotherapy." In *Women, Girls & Psychotherapy: Reframing Resistance*. Eds. C. Gilligan, A. Rogers, & D. Tolman. New York: The Haworth Press, 1991, 255.

16. Rich, *Taking Women Students Seriously*.

17. Hall, D. & S. Chimming. *Education for Change: A Workshop to Combat Sexual Harassment*. Workshop conducted at the conference on Sex/Race/Class Equity. Toronto: York University, 1990.

18. American Association of University Women, *Hostile Hallways: The AAUW Survey on Sexual Harassment in America's Schools*.

19. Herbert, C. Talking of Silence: The Sexual Harassment of Schoolgirls. London: The Falmer Press, 1989, 34.

20. Miller, *Towards a New Psychology of Women*, 54.

21. Ibid.

22. Maccoby, E. "Gender and Relationships: A Developmental Account," *American Psychologist* 45, 4 (1990), 514.

23. Ibid, p. 516.

24. Herbert, *"Talking of Silence: The Sexual Harassment of Schoolgirls,"* 88.

CHAPTER SIX

1. Staton and Larkin, *Sexual Harassment: The Intimidation Factor*.

2. Shoop & Hayhow, *Sexual Harassment in our Schools: What Parents and Teachers Need to Know to Spot it and Stop it*.

3. Crozier, K. "How Teenagers Can Fight Harassment in their Schools." *The Toronto Star* (25 July 1994), A15.

4. Boyd, *How One Teen Fought Sex Harassment in School,* 12.

5. Shoop & Hayhow, *Sexual Harassment in our Schools: What Parents and Teachers Need to Know to Spot it and Stop it,* 175.

6. Raymond, J. *A Passion for Friends.* Boston: Beacon Press, 1986, 8.

7. Frye, M. *The Politics of Reality: Essays in Feminist Theory.* Freedom, California: The Crossing Press, 1983, 38.

8. See, for example, Emerson, M. "Girls and Schooling Today." Presentation made to the Canadian Association of University Women. Markham, 1994; Sarah, E, M. Scott, and D. Spender. "The Education of Feminists: The Case for Single-Sex Schools." In *Learning to Lose: Sexism in Education.* Revised edition. Eds. E. Sarah and D. Spender. London: The Women's Press, 1988, 55-66; Yates, L. "Is Girl Friendly Schooling Really What We Need?" In *Girl Friendly Schooling.* Ed. J. Whyte. London: Methuen, 1985, 209-230.

9. Lewington, J. "Pioneering Parents Push for More Choices in Schools." *Globe and Mail* (7 April 1994): C1.

10. Mahony, *Sexual Violence in a Mixed Secondary School,* 181.

11. Ibid.

12. Battersea County Women's Group. "A School Experience: Implementing Equality in a Mixed Comprehensive School." In *Just a Bunch of Girls.* Ed. G. Weiner. Philadelphia: Milton Keynes, 1985, 130.

13. Naveau, B. "We Have a Lot to Say: Young Women for Gender Equity." *Canadian Woman Studies/les cahiers de la femme* 12, 3 (1992), 85.

14. Ibid, p. 86.

15. Gilligan, *Teachng Shakespeare's Sister: Notes from the Underground of Female Adolescence,* p. 27.

CONCLUSION

1. Stein, N. "It Happens Here Too: Sexual Harassment in the Schools". *Education Week* (27 November 1991), 25.

BIBLIOGRAPHY

American Association of University Women. *Hostile Hallways: The AAUW Survey on Sexual Harassment in America's Schools*. Louis Harris and Associates, Ltd, 1993.

American Association of University Women. *Shortchanging Girls: Shortchanging America*. Greenberg Lake: The Analyses Group Incorporated, 1990.

Adair, C.S. "When the Body Speaks: Girls, Eating Disorders & Psychotherapy." In *Women, Girls & Psychotherapy: Reframing Resistance*. Eds. C. Gilligan, A. Rogers, and D. Tolman, 253-266. New York: The Haworth Press, 1991.

Backhouse, C., and L. Cohen. *The Secret Oppression*. Toronto: MacMillan, 1978.

Bailey, K. *The Girls are the Ones with the Pointy Nails: An Exploration of Children's Conceptions of Gender*. London: The Althouse Press, 1993.

Bateman, P. "The Context of Date Rape." In *Dating Violence: Young Women in Danger*. Ed. B. Levy, 94-99. Seattle: The Seal Press, 1991.

Battersea County Women's Group. "A School Experience: Implementing Equality in a Mixed Comprehensive School." In *Just a Bunch of Girls*. Ed. G. Weiner. Philadelphia: Milton Keynes, 1985.

Belenky, M., B. Clinchy, N. Goldberger, and J. Tarule. *Women's Ways of Knowing: The Development of Self, Voice and Mind*. New York: Basic Books, 1986.

Boyd, C. "How One Teen Fought Sex Harassment in School." *St. Paul Pioneer Press*. (29 December 1991): 12.

Brickman, J., and J. Briere. "Incidents of Rape and Sexual Assault in Urban Canadian Population," *International Journal of Women's Studies* 7, 3 (1984): 195-206.

Briere, J., and N. Malamouth, N. "Self-reported Likelihood of Sexually Aggressive Behavior: An Attitudinal vs. Sexual Explanation," *Journal of Research and Personality* 17 (1983): 315-323.

Brown, L.M., and C. Gilligan. *Meeting at the Crossroads: Women's Psychology and Girls' Development.* Cambridge: Harvard University Press, 1992.

Bulzarik, M. "Sexual Harassment in the Workplace: Historical Notes," *Radical America* 12, (July-August 1978): 25-43.

Caplan, P., and J. Caplan. *Thinking Critically About Research on Sex and Gender.* New York: HarperCollins, 1993

Coulter, R. "Gender Socialization: New Ways, New World." Paper prepared for the Working Group of Status of Women Officials on Gender Equity in Education and Training, 1993.

Crozier, K. "How Teenagers Can Fight Harassment in Their Schools." *The Toronto Star* (25 July 1994), A15.

Dagg, A., and P. Thompson. *MisEducation: Women & Canadian Universities.* Toronto: OISE Press, 1988.

Eakins, B., and R.G. Eakins. *Sex Differences in Human Communication.* Boston: Houghton Mifflin, 1978.

Emerson, M. "Girls and Schooling Today." Presentation made to the Canadian Association of University Women. Markham, 1994.

Eyre, L. "Misogyny in the Classroom." Paper presented at the Canadian Women's Studies Association of the Learned Societies. Kingston, 1991.

Feldman, W., P. McGrath, and M. O'Shaughnessy. "Adolescents' Pursuit of Thinness." Abstracted, *American Journal of Dis Child* 140 (1986): 294.

Fraser, M.B. "Growing Up in a Sexual Jungle," *Canadian Woman Studies/les cahiers de la femme* 11, 4 (1991): 20-21.

Frye, M. *The Politics of Reality: Essays in Feminist Theory.* Freedom, CA: The Crossing Press, 1983.

Gaskell, J., A. McLaren, and M. Novogrodsky. *Claiming an Education: Feminism and Canadian Schools.* Toronto: Our Schools/Our Selves Education Foundation, 1989.

Gilligan, C. "Prologue." In *Making Connections: The Relational Worlds of Adolescent Girls at Emma Willard School.* Eds. C. Gilligan, N. Lyons, and T. Hanmer, 1-5. Cambridge: Harvard University Press, 1990.

Gilligan, C. "Teaching Shakespeare's Sister: Notes from the Underground of Female Adolescence." In *Making Connections: The Relational Worlds of Adolescent Girls at Emma Willard School* Eds. C. Gilligan, N. Lyons, and T. Hanmer, 6-29. Cambridge: Harvard University Press, 1990.

Gutek, B. *Sex and the Workplace.* San Francisco: Jossey-Bass Publishers, 1985.

Hall, D. and S. Chimming. *Education for Change: A Workshop to Combat Sexual Harassment.* Workshop conducted at the conference on Sex/Race/Class Equity. Toronto: York University, 1990.

Halson, J. The Sexual Harassment of Young Women. In *Girls and Sexuality: Teaching and Learning* Ed. L. Holly, 130-142. Philadelphia: Open University Press, 1988.

Haynes, P. Letter to Paula J. Caplan, 1991.

Herbert, C. *Talking of Silence: The Sexual Harassment of Schoolgirls.* London: The Falmer Press, 1989.

Houston, B. "What's Wrong with Sexual Harassment?" *Atlantis* 13, 2 (1988): 44-47.

Iversen, H. Personal communication, 1990.

Kelly, L. "The Continuum of Sexual Violence." In *Women, Violence and Social Control.* Ed. J. Hanmer and M. Maynard, 114-132. Beverly Hills: Sage, 1987.

Kelly, L. *Surviving Sexual Violence.* Minnesota: University of Minnesota Press, 1988.

Kimball, M. "Saying the Truth: Feminist Empiricism and the Work of Helen Thompson Woolley and Leta Stetter Hollingworth." Paper presented at the Canadian Psychology Meeting, Halifax, 1989.

Koss, M. "Changed Lives: The Psychological Impact of Sexual Harassment." In *Ivory Power: Sexual Harassment on Campus.* Ed. M. Paludi, 73-92. Albany: SUNY Press, 1990.

Levy, B. *Dating Violence: Young Women in Danger.* Seattle: The Seal Press, 1991.

Lewington, J. "Pioneering Parents Push for More Choices in Schools." *Globe and Mail* (7 April 1994): C1.

Lips, H. *Sex and Gender: An Introduction.* California: Mayfield Publishing Co., 1993.

Maccoby, E. "Gender and Relationships: A Developmental Account," *American Psychologist* 45, 4 (1990): 513-520.

MacKinnon, C. *Sexual Harassment of Working Women: A Case of Sex Discrimination.* New Haven, CT: Yale University Press, 1979.

Mahony, P. "Sexual Violence in a Mixed Secondary School." In *Learning our Lines.* Eds. C. Jones and P. Mahony, 157-190. London: The Women's Press, 1989.

Mann, J. *The Washington Post.* (6 May 1988).

Mercer, S. "Not a Pretty Picture: An Exploratory Study of Violence Against Women in Dating Relationships." *Resources for Feminist Research* (June, 1988): 15-22.

Merit Systems Protection Board. *Sexual Harassment in the Workplace: Is it a Problem?* Office of Merit Systems Review and Studies, Washington, DC: United States Government Printing Office, 1981.

Miller, B., and J. Marshall. "Coercive Sex on the University Campus." *Journal of College Student Personnel* 28, 1 (1987): 38-47.

Miller, J. "The Construction of Anger in Women and Men." In *Woman's Growth in Connection: Writings from the Stone Center.* Eds. J. Jordan, A. Kaplan, J. Baker Miller, I. Stiver, and J. Surrey, 181-196. New York: Guilford Press, 1991.

Miller, J. *Towards a New Psychology of Women* 2nd edition. Boston: Beacon Press, 1986.

Naveau, B. "We Have a Lot to Say: Young Women for Gender Equity." *Canadian Woman Studies/les cahiers de la femme* 12, 3 (1992):86-87.

Observer Review. "Masters Must Learn that Boys will be Brutes." (6 March 1994): 24.

Pharr, S. *Homophobia: A Weapon of Sexism.* Arkansas: Chardon Press, 1988.

Pleck, J. *Working Wives/Working Husbands.* Beverly Hills, CA: Sage, 1985.

Popaleni, K. "Violence Against Young Women in Heterosexual Courtship: Teaching Girls to Resist." *Canadian Woman Studies/les cahiers de la femme* 12, 1 (1991): 84-86.

Popaleni, K. "The Denial of the Self: An Exploratory Study of Young Women's Experiences of Violation within Heterosexual Courtship." Masters of Arts Thesis, University of Toronto, 1990.

Prose, F. "Confident at 11, Confused at 16." *New York Times* (7 January 1990): 24, 40.

Ramazanoglu, C. "Sex and Violence in Academic Life or You Can Keep a Good Woman Down." In *Women, Violence and Social Control.* Eds. J. Hanmer and M. Maynard, 61-74. London: MacMillan, 1987.

Randall, M. *Sexual Harassment.* Toronto: Ontario Women's Directorate, 1987.

Raymond, J. *A Passion for Friends.* Boston: Beacon Press, 1986.

Rich, A. "Taking Women Students Seriously." In *Lies, Secrets, and Silence,* 237-245. New York: Norton, 1979.

Ross, V., and J. Marlowe. *The Forbidden Apple: Sex in the Schools.* Palm Springs: ETC Publications, 1985.

Sadker, M., and D. Sadker. *Failing at Fairness: How America's Schools Cheat Girls.* New York: Charles Scribner's Sons, 1994.

Safran, C. "What Men do to Women on the Job. A Shocking Look at Sexual Harassment." *Redbook Magazine* (November, 1986): 149, 217.

Sarah, E, M. Scott, and D. Spender. "The Education of Feminists: The Case for Single-Sex Schools." In *Learning to Lose: Sexism in Education.* Revised edition. Eds. E. Sarah and D. Spender, 55-66. London: The Women's Press, 1988.

Shakeshaft, C. "A Gender at Risk." *Phi Delta Kappan* (March, 1986): 499-503.

Shields, S. "Functionalism, Darwinism, and the Psychology of Women: A Study in Social Myth." Reprinted in *Seldom Seen, Rarely Heard: Women's Place in Psychology.* Ed. J. Bohan, 79-106. Boulder: Westview Press, 1992.

Shoop, R. and Hayhow, J. *Sexual Harassment in Our Schools: What Parents and Teachers Need to Know to Spot it and Stop it.* MA: Allyn & Bacon, 1994.

Spender, D. "Gender and Marketable Skills: Who Underachieves in Maths and Sciences." In *Learning to Lose: Sexism in Education.* Eds. D. Spender and E. Sarah, 128-130. London: The Women's Press, 1988.

Spender, D. *Man-made Language.* London: Routledge & Kegan Paul, 1980.

Stanko, E. *Intimate Intrusions.* London: Routledge & Kegan Paul, 1986.

Staton, P., and J. Larkin. *Sexual Harassment: The Intimidation Factor.* A Report to the Ontario Ministry of Education, 1992.

Stein, N. "Secrets in Public: Sexual Harassment in Public (and Private) Schools." *Work Paper #256.* Wellesley, MA : Center for Research on Women, 1993.

Stein, N., N. Marshall, and L. Tropp. "Secrets in Public: Sexual Harassment in Our Schools." Wellesley, MA.: Center for Research on Women at Wellesley College and the NOW Legal Defense and Education Fund, 1993.

Stein, N. "It Happens Here Too: Sexual Harassment in the Schools." *Education Week* (27 November 1991): 32, 25.

Stein, N., ed. *Who's Hurt and Who's Liable: Sexual Harassment in Massachusett's Schools.* Quincy, MA: Massachusetts Department of Education, 1986.

Surrey, J. "Eating Patterns as a Reflection of Woman's Development." In *Woman's Growth in Connections: Writings from the Stone Center.* Eds. J. Jordan, A. Kaplan, J. Baker Miller, I. Stiver, and J. Surrey, 181-196. New York: The Guilford Press, 1991.

Tavris, C. *The Mismeasure of Woman.* New York: Simon & Schuster, 1992.

Walker, W. "Boyd: Sex Harassment Starts in our Schools." *The Toronto Star* (3 May 1994): A1.

Whitbread, A. "Female Teachers are Women First: Sexual Harassment at Work." In *Learning to Lose: Sexism and Education* Eds. D. Spender and E. Sarah, 90-96. London: The Women's Press, 1980.

Wise, S., and L. Stanley. *Georgie Porgie: Sexual Harassment in Everyday Life.* London: Pandora Press, 1987.

Woolley, H. "The Psychology of Sex." *Psychological* Bulletin 11 (1914): 353-379.

Yates, L. "Is Girl Friendly Schooling Really What We Need?" In *Girl Friendly Schooling.* Ed. J. Whyte, 209-230. London: Methuen, 1985.

OTHER BOOKS FROM SECOND STORY PRESS